HEAVE

ENCOUNTERS SERIES: Volume 1

A MEETING PLACE WITH GOD

YOUR PURPOSE AND DESTINY REVEALED

KEVIN L. ZADAI

WARRIORNOTES

DEDICATION

I dedicate this to the Lord Jesus Christ. He insisted that I go back and help people with their destinies. Because of Jesus's love and concern for people, He would actually send someone back to let them know that their destiny and purpose is secure in Him. I want you to know Lord, that when You come to take me to be with you someday, I hope that people remember the revelation of Jesus Christ and not me. I am merely being obedient to the heavenly calling and mission of my Lord, Jesus.

Table of Contents

ACKNOWLEDGMENTS

In addition to sharing my story with everyone through the book, "Heavenly Visitation: A Guide to the Supernatural" and "Days of Heaven on Earth: A Guide to the Days Ahead", the Lord gave me a commission to produce this book, *A Meeting Place With God*. It is a book that addresses some of the revelations concerning the areas that Jesus reviewed and revealed to me, in the Word of God and by the Spirit of God, during several visitations. I want to thank everyone who has encouraged me, assisted me, and prayed for me during the writing of this work, especially my spiritual parents, Dr. Jesse Duplantis and Dr. Cathy Duplantis. Special thanks to my wonderful wife Kathi, for her love and dedication to the Lord and me. Thank you, Sid Roth and staff, for your love of the our supernatural Messiah, Jesus. Thank you, Dr. Janet Kline for the wonderful job editing this book. Thank you, Mike and Lisa Houston for your support of this project. Special thanks, as well, to all my friends who know how to pray and enter into *A Meeting Place with God.*

Chapter 1

The Angel Escort

HEAVENLY MILITARY

*S*ometimes, we find ourselves in a transition period in life. We sense that there is more than we can see or hear, more completely what God has for us, but we don't seem to be able to enter fully into the revelation He is giving, or participate in it totally. This is known as a period of transition.

Angels are especially assigned to escort people into their destinies. If you feel that you are in this period in your life called "transition", then this chapter is for you! I felt that I should include this chapter concerning angels in the book because angels play an important part in arranging a meeting place with God. I will begin with the subject of angels and their role in our transition.

Right now, a lot of people are in transition because God is beginning to pour out His Spirit in a greater measure than ever before this time. The next wave of God's presence and glory are upon us.

Angels have many types of assignments. In this chapter, we are going to concentrate on their role in escorting you into your destiny. This may include a desert environment for many of you. A similar situation in the Old Testament where God's people were in a desert environment was when the children of Israel left Egypt and traveled through the desert. The angel of the Lord was sent on many occasions in the Bible.

Angels are sent to protect, give instructions, minister and strengthen, drive out the enemy, and to go before God's people to lead them. We need to pay attention and obey the instructions of these heavenly beings because they are among us right now. Here is the message Moses received from God and delivered to the people. We can learn much from studying the message that Moses spoke to Israel.

HOLY GROUND

So remember, angels are sent to help you in your transition and to make sure that you learn along the way. Angels are a vital part and help to arrange your meeting place with God. Remember a meeting place does not have to be a church building. Moses met an angel in the burning bush; he was asked to remove his sandals because he was standing on holy ground. When angels show up, the place where you are standing becomes a meeting place with God. Here is the account of what happened to Moses:

> And the Angel of the Lord appeared to him in a flame of fire from the midst of a bush. So he looked, and behold, the bush was burning with fire, but the bush was not consumed. Then Moses said, "I will now turn aside and see this great sight, why the bush does not burn." So when the Lord saw that he turned aside to look, God called to him from the midst of the bush and said,

"Moses, Moses!" And he said, "Here I am." Then He said, "Do not draw near this place. Take your sandals off your feet, for the place where you stand is holy ground (Exodus 3:2-5).

The main text for this chapter is in the book of Exodus. Moses was given very detailed instructions that have to do with the angel that was sent to escort them into the Promise Land. What many of people miss in this passage is the revelation of the character and duties of the holy ones called angels.

From this passage of scripture, we are going to glean the jewels of God's treasure chest, which are the mysteries and revelation about your destiny and purpose. Everything that is promised in the Word of God is for you. Angels have always been created for, and assigned for, specific purposes; their function has never changed. Their assignments are still effective today in getting you to the place called Destiny.

I am sending an **angel** before you **to protect** you on your journey and lead you safely to the place I have prepared for you. **Pay close attention to him, and obey his instructions.** Do not rebel against him, **for he is my representative**, and he will not forgive your rebellion. But if you are **careful to obey him, following all my instructions,** then I will be an enemy to your enemies, and I will oppose those who oppose you. For my angel will go before you and bring you into the land of the Amorites, Hittites, Perizzites, Canaanites, Hivites, and Jebusites, so you may live there. And I will destroy them completely. You must not worship the gods of these nations or serve them in any way or imitate their evil practices. Instead, you must utterly destroy them and smash their sacred pillars. "You must serve only the Lord your God. If you do, **I will bless you with food and water**, and **I will protect you from illness**. There will be no miscarriages or infertility in your land, and **I will give you long, full lives. I will send my terror ahead** of you and **create panic among all the people whose lands you invade. I will make all your enemies turn and run. I will send terror ahead of you to drive out** the Hivites, Canaanites, and Hittites (Exodus 23:20-29 NLT emphasis added).

SECRET AGENTS OF TRANSITION

Let's go over the specific assignments of angels who are with you. During transition, angels take you from where you happen to be at the time, to the point of your arrival at your rightful place in your purpose and destiny. There are some important revealed assets that you have because of these angels being assigned to you. Listed below are twenty assets that belong to you due to these assigned supernatural beings. We will be referring back to Exodus 23:20-29, as we study verse by verse about our meeting place concerning angel escort.

GOD'S MESSAGE TO HIS PEOPLE:
I AM SENDING MY ANGEL AHEAD OF YOU.
THANK YOU, LORD, FOR MY
ANGEL ESCORTS!

Here are the angel's duties and character traits under the instruction of Jesus Christ, their Commander:

1.   ANGELS ARE YOUR PROTECTORS

"To **protect** you on your
journey (Exodus 23:20a NLT emphasis added)."

As you begin your quest to know God's destiny for your life, you may have a journey upon which you will embark. Your "experience" of the journey will reveal your character as well as your Creator. Often, for the truths of our experiences to saturate our entire being and to reside deep within us, we must go through certain difficult challenges. It is not enough to just to experience something, it must change us not temporarily, but permanently, as well. Truth can be revealed, but it must also be experienced to glorify the Living God, who manifests Himself through us to the world. We are in this world, but not of it. (See John 17:16). We are just passing through this life. However, we live on the earth by faith. That faith must manifest to be complete. It is not enough to say we believe something. Our faith must manifest in this realm to complete the cycle of seed-time and harvest.

It is the same with you. You are on a journey to your destiny. It is a journey of faith. Your destiny must manifest, and not just be truth in the realm of the Spirit. Angels are your protectors along the way. They are absolutely overjoyed that God has chosen you for His purpose. They want to see that purpose fully manifest.

2.   YOUR ANGELS SAFELY LEAD YOU TO YOUR DESTINY

"To **lead** you safely to the place I have prepared for you (Exodus 23:20b NLT emphasis added)."

How exciting it is to think about this revealed truth. We actually have these wonderful "ministers of fire" standing with us and leading us safely to our special destiny that God has prepared. The loving

Father-God cares about you and your destiny. He has assigned these holy ones to make sure we get to our destination, which was prepared for us before we were born. It was prepared before the foundation of the earth.

3. ANGELS EXPECT YOU TO BE ATTENTIVE

"Pay close **attention** to him(Exodus 23:21a NLT emphasis added)."

God requires that we pay close attention to Him and His Word. We must not get our attention distracted by the world in our daily activities. We must pay close attention to what is going on around us in the spirit realm. Angels have a vital part of our life as we seek to know Jesus in a greater manner. We are not to seek angelic experiences. However, the supernatural should be part of our everyday experience.

4. ANGELS LOVE IT WHEN YOU ARE OBEDIENT

"**Obey** his instructions(Exodus 23:21b NLT emphasis   added)."

As we know, throughout the Bible the Lord asks us to harken unto His voice. As God reveals Himself to man, the most important element to remember is that God says to hear His voice and obey. God's plans and purposes for you are dependent upon your hearing the instructions that are given in the Word of God and obeying them. When an angel is sent as an ambassador of God, it is often for the purpose of delivering a message or for implementing God's will. Sometimes, His Word comes through angels as they carry out His will on the earth. Angels constantly hear God and obey God. Angels expect you also to hear and to obey God. That is why God said that you are to obey what the angel says.

5. ANGELS HATE REBELLION

"Do not **rebel** against him (Exodus 23:21c NLT emphasis added)."

There can potentially be all kinds of different reactions that occur when God speaks into someone's life. Those reactions can, in part, be determined by the person's present understanding of spiritual things, as well as other influences in his or her life. The Word of God is always true. We are expected to obey His Word. The Bible says that rebellion is as a sin of witchcraft. If a person's heart is not right toward God, he or she will reject what is being said and done. Angels cannot work when there is rebellion. They hate it when people are being rebellious to God's instruction. They hate what God hates, and God hates rebellion. So the Lord warns His people not to rebel against the angels who are doing His work. If you want the will of God in your life, and want to fulfill your purpose and destiny, then you must not rebel against God or His angels. They are working to accomplish all that is in God's heart for you. You must cooperate with the instructions that angels give because those instructions originate in God. We must learn to yield to the Spirit realm.

6. ANGEL'S ARE GOD'S REPRESENTATIVES

"He is my **representative** (Exodus 23:21d NLT emphasis added)."

When we realize that angels are sent as ambassadors or representatives, we must realize that the way that we treat angels is a reflection of how we treat God. They come to promote the kingdom of God and enforce the government of God through righteousness, peace, holiness, and joy in the Holy Spirit. Whatever you do to angels, who are essentially God's representatives, you are therefore also doing to the Lord. Even children are not to be offended (see Matthew 18:10). Their angels always see the face of their Father in heaven. You will get reported to God if you harm a child. When angels are sent to us, we respect them as God's representatives. We must be open to the Word of the Lord that could come forth from there mouths.

7. ANGELS HAVE NO FORGIVENESS FOR REBELLION

"He will not forgive your rebellion (Exodus 23:21e NLT emphasis added)."

The bottom line of rebellion is this one: it is the same as operating as a witch. If you are going to rebel against the plans and purposes of God for your life and for those of the others around you, the angels will have no forgiveness for you. You may get right with God, but you do not want to offend the angels. We need to walk in love toward our brother or sister and forgive, but not rebel. The Lord will never withhold anything from you. Everyone must forgive, let go of offenses, and walk in love toward

God and our fellow man. Then, and only then, the angels can be released to do their assigned work in our lives.

8.   DO WHAT ANGELS SAY

"Be careful to obey him, following all
My instructions (Exodus 23:22a NLT emphasis
added)."

Yes, you are on your way to your destiny. Make a conscious effort to hear what the Lord is saying through His Word and by His Spirit. The book of Proverbs is full of quotes concerning wisdom. God is often personified as wisdom. Wisdom is constantly asking the reader to hear His voice and follow His instructions (see Proverbs). When angels are assigned to escort you to your destiny and purpose, they are listening to the Word of our Lord. If they have any instructions for you along the way, you must follow them if you wish to fulfill God's destiny and purpose for your life.

9.   YOUR ENEMIES ARE GOD'S ENEMIES

"I will be an enemy to your enemies (Exodus
23:22b NLT emphasis added)."

As a child of God, you must receive full revelation from the Holy Spirit that God loves you beyond measure. Most people today do not operate in their full potential because they do not have this revelation. Those who have received this revelation have gone on to do exploits for God above and beyond what most people could possibly comprehend.

Part of the manifestation of God's love is His protection. He is very protective of His own, because we have been adopted into His family through Jesus Christ, He sets Himself against any of your enemies. We know that, according to His instructions to the children of Israel, we are joined together to form one family in Heaven and on earth. Therefore, if anyone becomes our enemy, God becomes their enemy also. Anyone who will fight against you because of your stand for God is actually fighting against God Himself. We're wrestling not against flesh and blood, but against these evil entities that are unseen (see Ephesians 6:12).

It is good to know that God is watching over us. Remember, however, we must call those whom He calls as His enemies our enemies also. We must call those whom He calls as His friends as our friends also.

10.   ANGELS WILL OPPOSE THOSE WHO GOD OPPOSES

"I will oppose those who oppose you (Exodus 23:22c NLT emphasis added)."

Angels receive orders from God Himself. If you find yourselves being a opposed by an enemy, be assured that the angels have been told to confront and fight against anyone or anything that opposes you. When you stand in your righteous authority and are walking with Him, Your enemies will find themselves working against God Himself and against angels.   Angels enforce God's justice in every situation. Whatsoever you may agree to honor, God will ensure it is also honored in Heaven. Angels are the ancient agents whose job is to enforce the choices that we make by the Spirit of God, according to the will of God.

Remember to walk in love towards everyone. Then, you cannot be implicated in any opposition. Be certain to drop any offenses and forgive any trespasses. This will keep the angels working quickly and efficiently. Make sure that the words of your mouth are pleasing in the sight of God and the angels. Then, He will be able to complete His perfect in your life.

11. ANGELS WILL BRING YOU INTO YOUR LAND

"For my angel will go before you and bring you into the land so you may live there (Exodus 23:23a NLT emphasis added)."

How exciting is this! This verse explains to us the angel escort going ahead of us. His goal is to bring you into the land, which is your destiny and purpose, so that you may live there. This is the Word of God, and what a promise it is to us. We are on our way. The Lord has sent His mighty servants to pave the way for us. Once again, I want to emphasize the fact that we are going into the land in which we will live. It is a good land that has all the provisions to help us fulfill our destiny and purpose in God through Jesus Christ. He has provided this for us through His shed blood.

12. ANGELS WILL DESTROY YOUR ENEMIES

" I will destroy them completely(Exodus 23:23b NLT emphasis added)."

It is a wonderful thing that God leads us into our land and pushes out our enemy, but He also promised the children of Israel that He would destroy our enemies. That means that we will never have to deal with them again. What Jesus Christ has done for us is a finished work. He came to "destroy the works of the devil (1 John 3:8 emphasis added)." He promises in Isaiah, "Say to those with fearful hearts, 'Be strong, and do not fear, for your God is coming to destroy your enemies. He is coming to save you (Isaiah 35:4). ' "

These angels of transition have created a meeting place with God, even in your journey. But eventually they're taking you to your land where a permanent meeting place with God can happen.

Angels do not have an opinion; they only do what God the Father has told them to do. If God says to destroy the works of the devil in combat, then they will do it. All we need to do is pray, agree, and stand in faith, declaring the Word of the Lord. Then everything will come out exactly how it is supposed to be.

13.   DESTROY PAGAN ALTARS

"You must not worship the gods of these nations or serve them in any way or imitate their evil practices. Instead, you must utterly destroy them and smash their sacred pillars (Exodus 23:24 NLT emphasis added)."

We must remember that we have responsibilities as well as the angels. There are certain things that are our responsibility to perform, and that angels do not have responsibility to do. One of the Commandments that God told Moses to tell the people was that they were not to worship any gods beside Him. They were not to serve these gods of other nations in anyway or to imitate their evil practices. This is stated in Exodus.

But God goes even a step further than most of us would go today. God told the children of Israel to destroy all. This included smashing and destroying all symbols of their gods. It was not enough to exclude their practices. They were to completely rid the land of anything profane.

This was a radical step, but this is what the Lord asked them to do, along with what the angels were doing. It is very important to understand that we are working with angels. They are aware that we must do our part. The angels know that we have certain assignments that we must fulfill in order for God's perfect will to come to pass in our lives.

It's interesting to know that even if angels have done their part, we still have responsibilities in order to fulfill God's perfect will. There is order in heaven. We have a covenant with God that angels do not. We represent God's authority on this earth. We must implement certain things in order for God to be free to act on our behalf.

14.   SERVE GOD ONLY

"You must serve only the Lord your
God (Exodus 23:25a NLT emphasis added)."

Please remember that we must continually remind ourselves who God is and whom we serve. We must not let this world or its system distort the truth that originated from Heaven. All the plans and purposes of God are written in Heaven. Holy men of old were moved by the Holy Ghost and wrote and spoke the Word of God (2 Peter1:21). We must continually remind ourselves of what is true and not judge the world's "facts" as truth. We are in this world, but not of it. We must serve God with all our being in order to display His glory on the earth.

15.   GOD WILL BLESS YOU SUPPLIES

"I will bless you with food and water   (Exodus
23:25b NLT emphasis added)."

The character of God is so awesome. It is amazing to think that He could take us to our destiny and protect us, while at the same time creating a meeting place for us. But He also promises to bless us with all our provisions, such as food and water. With His blessing on these two things, there is no doubt that our day will be much more effective than those who do not have God's blessing. God is actively moving and maintaining your life in your land of destiny and purpose. You will not have to worry about these things as you serve Him with all of your heart and seek His kingdom (Matthew 6:33).

16.   GOD WILL KEEP YOU WELL

> "I will protect you from illness   (Exodus 23:25c
> NLT emphasis added)."

As well as providing you with all that you need for sustenance in your new land of destiny and purpose, God also offers healthcare in your new land. You will not get sick according to His Word here. Even in their transition in the desert, the people of God had everything they needed. Even their clothing did not wear out. Now He is saying that you will not have any illness because He will protect you from it.

17.   GOD WILL MULTIPLY YOU

> "There will be no miscarriages or infertility in your land.   (Exodus 23:26a NLT emphasis added)."

You will have no miscarriages nor be infertile in your land of destiny and purpose. This is both physical and spiritual for us. You will carry your vision to full fruition; it will not be miscarried. Everything that you touch shall prosper and produce all that you need. You will not be infertile. This is prosperity. This is multiplication. This is your new land called destiny and purpose.

18.   GOD WILL GIVE YOU LONG LIFE

> "I will give you long, full lives (Exodus 23:26b
> NLT emphasis added)."

As we keep on reading here in Exodus, the covenant of God gets better and better. The Lord now promises us not only quality of life, but the quantity of life. He says we will have a long life. Part of the blessing of the Lord is to live long and to prosper in the land that He has given. The angels will make sure that this happens. They will enforce the covenant that you have made with your God through Jesus Christ.

The longer that you live here on this earth, the longer you will have walked with your Creator in the power of the Spirit and revelation. You will learn the ways of God and walking in His authority, therefore, you will be very effective as your years increase. God needs people to walk in their authority with a long life to enforce the kingdom of God. He needs people walking in the authority He provides because His Kingdom is expanding at an alarming rate in the Spirit now.

19. GOD WILL SEND TERROR AHEAD OF YOU

"I will send my terror ahead of you and create panic among all the people whose lands you invade (Exodus 23:27a NLT emphasis added)."

Another interesting aspect of your journey, besides the fact that the angels are going ahead of you, is the aspect of filling the minds of the people that wrongfully occupy your property in your land, with terror. God creates a panic among them.

God is working and will prepare the way for the day that you invade, drive out, and cast out the enemy from the land of destiny and purpose that the Lord has provided. The fear of the Lord is the beginning of wisdom. But to the enemy, the fear of the Lord is a sign of the undoing of their power and possession. As God leads you there by His angels and by the Spirit of the living God, you will see the enemy vacate your land.

20.   GOD WILL DRIVE YOUR ENEMIES OUT

"I will make all your enemies turn and run. I will send terror ahead of you to drive out   (Exodus 23:27b NLT emphasis added)."

As you use the name of Jesus against your enemies, they will turn and run. Jesus clearly said that we will cast out devils, and that nothing shall by any means harm us (see Luke 10:19). It is exciting to see how the blessing of the Lord is enforced by the angels. Angels are continually working on our behalf in response to the Word of the Lord.

We should be encouraged, even during our time of transition through the desert, because we are going to our land, a land which has clearly been prepared for us. We should also be encouraged because we may participate in taking what God has promised us, even before we get there. God's Spirit and His angels are sustaining us even in hard times. Be encouraged because the angels want you to be blessed as much as you desire to be blessed. God loves you. God and His angels are here to help you.

FLAMES OF FIRE

"Regarding the angels, He says, "He sends his angels like the winds, His servants like **flames of fire** (Hebrews 1:7 NLT)."

"Therefore, angels are only servants— spirits sent to care for people who will inherit salvation

(Hebrews 1:14 NLT)."

Angels are "flames of fire" (see Psalm 104:4). They are sent to minister to those who are to inherit salvation (see Hebrews 1:14). These angels burn with the holy fire of God. They are so pure that when they are next to you, you cannot help but be overcome by the presence and environment of Heaven. They are messengers that minister destiny and purpose to you. When they show up, the will of God is done. However, you must cooperate for things to work out correctly. Angels are not just sent to deal with problems and conflicts that you have created in your own life. They are co-laborers with you. Angels help to fulfill the purposes and plans of God on the earth, which include those purposes and plans for your life.

Angels are very fast, very bright with God's glory, and very happy. Doing God's will is not only natural to an angel, but it is something that thrills them! They are so excited to please God and do His will.

> Now Moses was tending the flock of Jethro his father-in-law, the priest of Midian. And he led the flock to the back of the desert, and came to Horeb, the mountain of God. And the **Angel of the Lord appeared to him in a flame of fire** from the midst of a bush (Exodus 3:1-2 emphasis added).

The angels sometimes appear as a flames of fire. They are burning with God's Holy presence. The have a passion for God's Holy purposes on the earth. I have angelic activity around me continually and you do as well. I invite them to assist me and help me realize fully what God is presently working in my life. The fire that is on them is hot with the personality of God. His Holy presence can be encountered among them as the stand with you, as you minister for the

Lord. You actually feel like you are in Heaven when angels are around. You will feel enabled when they are near. Your destiny starts to unfold wherever angels are found.

The angel of the Lord and the Pillar of cloud and fire were two different things (see Exodus 14:19). God uses angels to bring a light to objects, such as the burning bush that Moses saw. At times when the angel would go behind the people, traveling to the Promise Land, the people would still have a pillar cloud. That cloud, either shaded them during the hot, desert days, or burned at night to light up the camp to protect them in the evening. From these truths, we can see that God has different ways to escort His own into our destinies.

EXCEL IN STRENGTH

"Bless the Lord, you His angels,
Who **excel in strength** (Psalm 103:20)."

One of the fascinating characteristics of angels that are escorting you during your transition is the strength in which they excel. Because they are completely coordinated with God in purpose and character, they excel in the area of strength. They are to be able to supersede this physical realm. This allows angels to bring victory on your behalf. Because angels are strong, they can protect you as well as make a way for you to succeed. The ability of angels to perform these things on your behalf creates a meeting place with God even during transition. During these times when we are in transition, the presence of angels make a very anointed time of victory. We know God is with us in our endeavor. But just remember, we are on our way to "the land that God has prepared for us." It is our land of destiny and purpose.

You do not have to see these angels to know that they are there. It is amazing. Angels carry such a presence with them. That presence begins in the Throne Room of God. God can strengthen you, just He did with Jesus when He was in the desert. It was His time of transition. He was evolving from being a Jewish boy to being a Jewish rabbi, anointed by the Holy Spirit with power. After being tempted in the desert, Jesus went out in power to destroy the works of the devil. Angels came to minister to Jesus after He was tempted by the devil. "Then the devil left Him, and behold, angels came and ministered to Him (Matthew 4:11)."

GOD'S VOICE

"**Heeding the voice** of His word (Psalm 103:20b)"

One amazing characteristic of angels is their complete devotion and obedience that angels have concerning the Word of God. When they hear the Lord speak, they do not argue or reason away what God has said. They simply do whatever the Lord has commanded. Angels have expressed to me the excitement that they have when people react in a similar way and completely obey the Lord. The angels are absolutely going to perform every single act that God tells them to do. It is of the utmost importance to them to hear the commands from Heaven and obey them. When we human beings also are totally obedient to God, it makes the work of angels much less difficult.

Angels love people who comprehend the ways of God and have no resistance towards God and His Word. There have been times when I have witnessed angels become enthralled when I myself, have obeyed the Lord willingly, without resisting His promptings. The angels' rejoicing at my obedience astonishes me at times. I like what the New Living Translation says about this verse, "So bless the Lord, all his messengers of power, for you are his mighty heroes who listen to the voice of His Word to do it (Psalms 103:20 NLT)!"

Angels know that God never fails; therefore, angels know that they are to listen to everything God says and completely carry out His commands. This is that for which angels live: to fulfill the instructions of the Lord. Angels recognize that if the human race will cooperate completely by following God's commands, then it will be possible for the kingdom of God to have complete victory in the earth. That is the reason a country completely changes and prospers: because the Christian church has begun to grow and supersede all power in that nation. The reason this works is because angels are in the midst of that church, and the Word of God can therefore produce fruit. The angels among that nation are creating destiny and purpose for that country and for the people of that country.

GOD'S WILL

"Yes, praise the Lord, you armies of angels
who serve him and **do His will** (Psalms 103:21)!"

Another amazing characteristic of angels is their ability to serve Him with all of their being. These mighty armies of angels serve God relentlessly, worshipping Him the whole time they are working for Him. They want to serve God and do His will. They are completely satisfied with serving God to the utmost. So if you desire to have angels be present with you at all times, you must have some character traits in your life in common with angels. We need to adopt certain essential traits. All of Heaven is serving God and doing His will, not their own purpose, but to help fulfill the purposes of God. We must learn to serve not our own will, but the will of the Lord.

This is why one large part of the Gospel message is "dying to yourself" and picking up "the cross and carrying it". The Apostle Paul said, " I have been **crucified** with Christ; it is no longer I who live, but Christ lives in me; and the life which I now live in the flesh I live **by faith** in the Son of God, who loved me and gave Himself for me (Galatians 2:20-21 emphasis added). God's will is perfect. Sometimes we humans need the Holy Spirit to help us be convinced that His will is perfect! When we have been firmly convinced that the Lord's will is perfect, we are more readily able to be crucified with Him and live by faith. Then we will do the will of God just as the angels do His will.

GOD'S PLEASURE

"Bless the Lord, all you His hosts,
You ministers of His, who do **His pleasure** (Psalms 103:21)."

God creates this wonderful atmosphere for you to meet with Him, even in transition times. God has mighty angelic hosts that do His pleasure. Think about it; they please God at all times and are always doing the things that please Him. Whatever it is that you are going through, remember that your angels are with you. They make God rejoice because they do everything that God desires. If you will allow these biblical truths to permeate your innermost being, you will begin to see the pleasure of the Lord come forth in your life in a greater measure than ever before now. You will not always be able to understand everything that is going on in your life, but you can always meet with God and gain understanding and guidance. This conversation can occur even if you are in transition to your destiny. Angels are a great part of ministering to, and for, all saints. They certainly have helped me on many occasions to have complete faith that God will fulfill His promises. At such times, angels ministered to give strength and guidance. It is important to remember to enjoy your time with God in this meeting place. Know that angels are a vital part of this time and are surrounding you on every side as you transition into your place of destiny and purpose in the "land that God has prepared for you.

Chapter 2

The Pillar Of Cloud

And the Angel of God, who went before the
camp of Israel, moved and went behind them; and the pillar
of cloud went from before them and stood behind them. So it
came between the camp of the Egyptians and the camp of
Israel. Thus it was a cloud and darkness to the one, and it
gave light by night to the other, so that the one did
not come near the other all that night
(Exodus 14:19-20).

The pillar cloud was with the children of Israel continually not just as a sign, but for their protection as well. The pillar cloud represented God's presence for His people as they were in the transition phase of their deliverance from Egypt. The cloud helped the people in the daytime and at night. It was a cloud that glowed at night as it burned with the glory of God. It provided daylight if there were enemies approaching or if they needed to travel at night. During the day, the cloud provided a visible sign that God was with them. Also, it provided shade from the scorching hot sun that shone on them in the desert. The pillar cloud and fire were also a meeting place with God. God creates a similar situation for us as we move about each day. He is guiding us into our place of destiny.

SIX FACTS ABOUT THE GLORY AND FIRE CLOUD

1. **Pillar of cloud and the pillar of fire guided them**. It allowed them to travel and be guided either day or night in the wilderness (see Exodus 13:21).

Because of our new walk with the Lord in the Spirit, we have the glory and the fire inside us, not just on us or around us. This is very important to remember. Jesus purchased our way into the Holy of Holies with His blood. Now that glory and fire are inside of us through the new birth.

BURNING BRIGHT

The Holy Spirit is burning bright. He is going ahead of you, as well as giving instruction inside your own spirit. We can be guided supernaturally everyday by the Holy Spirit inside us. Let the fire and glory of God lead you into your Land of Promise with Him. Your destiny involves the pillar of fire and glory.

2. **This pillar was always in front of them and was always visible,** except when they needed protection from the enemy. The approach of the enemy required the pillar to go behind them. It moved to that position to protect them. (see Exodus 13:22).

The pillar protected the children of God from the enemy. When you are in transition to your destiny, the enemy may confront you. He will do everything he can within his power to try to stop you. Just as the cloud of the fire and glory would go behind to protect the children of Israel, God will position His angels in the proper place to protect you.

When you are confronted, the pillar of fire and glory will become your rear guard in this special time with the Lord. "For you shall not go out with haste, nor go by flight; for the Lord will go before you, and the God of Israel will be your **rear guard** (Isaiah 52:12 emphasis added).

Rest assured that God is watching over you in this particular meeting place, in the desert phase of your life. He is testing you to see what is in you. He is training you to hear His voice in the desert. Then you will know Him as He meets with you. Then you will not be led astray by anything or anybody that is not of Him.

VOICES VS "THE VOICE"

There are many voices that attempt to be heard in our lives that are not correct. They are competing for your attention. The Lord will train you to hear the true voice of God and allow the truth to become part of your life permanently.

> If there arises among you a prophet or a dreamer of dreams, and he gives you a sign or a wonder, and the sign or the wonder comes to pass, of which he spoke to you, saying, 'Let us go after other gods' — which you have not known — 'and let us serve them,' you shall not listen to the words of that prophet or that dreamer of dreams, for the Lord your God is testing you to know whether you love the Lord your God with all your heart and with all your soul. You shall walk after the Lord your God and fear Him, and keep His commandments and obey His voice; you shall serve Him and hold fast to Him (Deuteronomy 13:1-5 emphasis added).

The voice of the Lord is the Spirit of Truth. The Spirit will help you discern what is truth and what is false. You will begin to "meditate on His Word day and night" (see Joshua 1:8). He will confirm His Word to you by the Spirit of Truth, who has been given to you as a guide. He will guide you into all truth (see John 16:13).

3. **The angel of God, and the Pillar of cloud and fire** were two different things (see Exodus 14:19).

The angels and the Pillar cloud are two separate entities that are provided for you in the desert, just as they were present to assist the children of Israel. God's presence is with you through the Holy Spirit. He is ever present to guide you. Angels are responsible for your escort and for your protection.

HEAVENLY STATEGIES

Remember that God told the Israelites not to grieve the angel who was responsible to keep them on the proper path. "Behold, I send an angel before thee, to keep thee in the way, and to bring thee into the place which I have prepared. Beware of him, and obey his voice, provoke him not; for he will not pardon your transgressions: for my name is in him (Exodus 23: 20,21 KJV)."

God's strategy is to guide you into your destiny. Along the way, He will also teach you obedience. He will perform this work within you as your travel through the desert. He will take this opportunity to develop your faith. Your faith is precious to God and will be rewarded. The Apostle Peter referred to the trials you may be facing and the faith that results when He said, "In this you greatly rejoice, though now for a little while, if need be, you have been grieved by various trials, that the genuineness of your faith, being much more precious than gold that perishes, though it is tested by fire, may be found to praise, honor, and glory at the revelation of Jesus Christ, whom having not seen, you love (1 Peter 1:6-8)."

So in this desert situation, God does not prevent certain events from happening, but protects and guides you through them. When you recognize that the circumstances that you face become a platform of divine strategy to produce faith, you will learn to let the process occur. Then, when you become mature enough to recognize the importance of overcoming circumstances to achieve victory, you will pass all of your faith tests.

After God brought the children of Israel out of Egypt, they rebelled. They did not enter into the Promise Land because of their unbelief. What will you learn from their experience? The writer of Hebrews was encouraging all readers to learn from this event so not one person would find himself or herself in the same situation of unbelief.

For who, having heard, rebelled? Indeed, was it not all who came out of Egypt, led by Moses? Now with whom was He angry forty years? Was it not with those who sinned, whose corpses fell in the wilderness? And to whom did He swear that they would not enter His rest, but to those who did not obey? So we see that they could not enter in because of unbelief. Therefore, since a promise remains of entering His rest, let us fear lest any of you seem to have come short of it. For indeed the gospel was preached to us as well as to them; but the word which they heard did not profit them, **not being mixed with faith in those who heard it** (emphasis added Hebrews 3:16-4:2).

We must allow this special meeting place in the desert with God to develop our faith and help to move you into your destiny. God and His angels want you to succeed. Heaven wants you to pass all of your tests, especially in this time of transition.

4. **God wanted to display His glory by using the "pillar and fire" against the enemy.** He wanted Pharaoh to chase them. God told Moses, "And once again I will harden Pharaoh's heart, and he will chase after you. **I have planned this in order to display my glory** through Pharaoh and his whole army. After this the Egyptians will know that I am the Lord!" So the Israelites camped there as they were told (Exodus 14:4 NLT emphasis added)."

GOD PICKS A FIGHT

The situation which involved the hardening of Pharaoh's heart towards the children of the Lord was a divine preparation that God orchestrated in order to display His glory to the enemy. Many times, we find ourselves getting nervous when God hardens our enemies' hearts and they start to chase us. At times such as these, it is essential that we trust in God and partner with Him in covenant. "And they overcame him by the blood of the Lamb and by the Word of their testimony, and they did not love their lives to the death (Revelation 12:11)." Our trust in Him is then strengthened when we have victory in our trials. When we do what pleases Him and pass our tests, He will certainly meet with us and answer all of our prayers. God announces through the Prophet Isaiah, "Then your light shall break forth like the morning, Your healing shall spring forth speedily, And your righteousness shall go before you; The glory of the Lord shall be your rear guard. Then you shall call, and the Lord will answer; You shall cry, and He will say, 'Here I am' (Isaiah 58:8-9 emphasis added)."

I have learned not to get into fear when certain scenarios begin to mount against God's destiny and purpose in my life.

I have realized that God is setting up the enemy for a battle that exposes the enemies' inability to win any fight against God's purposes in my life.

5. **God was in the fire and pillar cloud.** "But just before dawn the Lord looked down on the Egyptian army from **the pillar of fire and cloud, and He threw their forces into total confusion**. He twisted their chariot wheels, making their chariots difficult to drive. 'Let's get out of here—away from these Israelites!' the Egyptians shouted. 'The Lord is fighting for them against Egypt!' (Exodus 14:24-25 NLT emphasis added)."

GOD LOOKS DOWN

This is an exciting revelation of God's personality! He was in the pillar cloud of fire, and He looked down and saw the army that was gathered against His people. He knew how the enemy was attacking His own. He sent "total confusion" against the enemies. He even twisted their chariot wheels. As a result, the enemy realized that God Himself was fighting against them, so they tried to flee completely from Him.

God is setting you up for a victory in your time of transition. The enemy has lost you. You are never going back to him. Even if he chases after you, he will meet up with your God who has planned the victory to be completely in your favor.

6. **There was awesome glory displayed before God's people**. "As Aaron spoke to the whole community of Israel, they looked out toward the wilderness. There they could see **the awesome glory of the Lord in the cloud** (Exodus 16:10 NLT emphasis added)."

AWESOME GLORY

One thing have I desired of the Lord,
that will I seek after; that I may dwell in the house of the Lord
all the days of my life, to behold the beauty of the Lord,
and to inquire in his temple (Psalm 27:4 KJV).

The Lord desires to display His glory in front of His people so that they may behold his beauty. He longs for us to seek after Him as King David spoke of seeking after Him. Let us not hold back. Those who cry out for Him will see that God will come and display His glory to His people.

Let us seek the one true God, Jesus Christ our Savior. May the Spirit of revelation open our eyes to see the inheritance that we have in the Saints (see Ephesians 1:17-23). We cannot hold back any longer. We must cry out to Him. We need a full revelation of Jesus Christ. We need to see His glory manifest in our lives.

There is no greater desire deep within a believer's heart than to behold and gaze upon the beauty of the Lord. Just remember that we must continue to express our desire to know Him in a deep and intimate way. Continue to ask of Him and seek Him, for if you do, He will answer. The Lord Jesus in all His glory is such a sight to behold. I have seen Him in all His glory; I am overcome when His presence and His glory appear. Let us continue to meditate and consider His beauty as we meet with Him in the various places and in the various ways He brings such glory to our lives.

Chapter 3

The Mountain

Be ready and come up in
the morning to Mount Sinai, **and present
yourself there to Me on the top of the
mountain** (Exodus 34:2 AMP).

We should always be ready for the moment when God
calls us to be alone with Him. You may be as Moses, called
to the mountain far away from everyone. Up there on a
mountain, He seems so detached from the world. When we
are alone and in an isolated position, it helps us to focus on
God alone.

We all need a mountain experience at least once in our
lives with God. God alone calls us, and God alone sustains
us. Sometimes without knowing we are called by God and
He is the One who sustains us, we start to depend upon the
people around us and the system of this world. We forget
some of the simple truths that God has revealed in our
previous journeys.

The children of Israel found themselves at the foot of

Mount Sinai. Their transition into the Promised Land, which was their destiny and purpose, was delayed because of their unbelief. God had asked all the people to come up and meet with Him. They refused because they were afraid. So Moses went up and encountered God alone, face-to-face. The Lord was upset with the people because they would not come up to be in fellowship with Him. Therefore, in His anger He set borders around the mountain so that only Moses was allowed to come to the mountaintop. Moses found himself defending the people because God had brought them out and now He was upset with them. Moses interceded for the people, and God accepted the desires of Moses to be merciful to them.

Moses was asking God to show him even more of Himself. He wanted to know His ways. Such desire as Moses possessed is a key to being on the mountain and meeting with God.

> One day Moses said to the Lord, "You have been telling me, 'Take these people up to the Promised Land.' But you haven't told me whom you will send with me. You have told me, 'I know you by name, and I look favorably on you.' If it is true that you look favorably on me, let me know your ways so I may understand you more fully and continue to enjoy your favor. And remember that this nation is your very own people. "The Lord replied, "I will personally go with you, Moses, and I will give you rest—everything will be fine for you. "Then Moses said, "If you don't personally go with us, don't make us leave this place. How will anyone know that you look favorably on me—on me and on your people—if you don't go with us? For your presence among us sets your people and me apart from all other people on the earth. "The

Lord replied to Moses, "I will indeed do what you have asked, for I look favorably on you, and I know you by name. "Moses responded, "Then show me your glorious presence. "The Lord replied, "I will make all my goodness pass before you, and I will call out my name, Yahweh, before you. For I will show mercy to anyone I choose, and I will show compassion to anyone I choose. But you may not look directly at my face, for no one may see me and live." The Lord continued, "Look, stand near me on this rock. As my glorious presence passes by, I will hide you in the crevice of the rock and cover you with my hand until I have passed by. Then I will remove my hand and let you see me from behind. But my face will not be seen (Exodus 33:12-23 NLT)."

1. **The Cloud.**

The mountain was a good place for God to visit with Moses. He chose the mountain because of the isolation the mountain afforded the opportunity to have privacy with Moses. Another special element in this situation was that God chose to speak to Moses from a cloud. God also displayed great respect for Moses.

The children of Israel were in disobedience because they were supposed to come with Moses and encounter visitation on the mountain. The Lord said to Moses, "I will come to you in a **thick cloud**, Moses, so **the people themselves can hear me when I speak with you**. Then they will always trust you (Exodus 19:9 NLT emphasis added)".

So the children of Israel missed a tremendous opportunity to experience the Lord because they did not accept the invitation to go up and meet with God face-to-face. This caused them to be constantly on the outside looking in, just as the religious people of today. The children totally missed out on the supernatural relationship you can have with God. People of today also can completely miss the opportunity to be with God. People such as these fail to realize that they, too, can have their meeting place with God.

Moses was told by God, " And no man shall come up with you, neither let any man be seen throughout all the mountain; neither let flocks or herds feed before that mountain (Exodus 34:3 AMP)."

It is amazing how much God does for people that others do not always discern. He honestly has given people the way to meet with Him. People want things to be done their way, instead of the way that God desires. Jesus is the only way, and He is the new and living way. We can enter in through Him, and Him alone.

For those who choose to go to the meeting place with God on the mountain, many wonderful truths will be revealed. Moses obeyed and when up. This is what happened.

> And the Lord descended in the cloud and stood with him there and proclaimed the name of the Lord. And the Lord passed by before him, and proclaimed, The Lord! the Lord! a God merciful and gracious, slow to anger, and abundant in loving-kindness and truth, keeping mercy and loving-kindness for thousands, forgiving iniquity and transgression and sin, but Who will by no means clear the guilty, visiting the iniquity of the fathers upon the children and the children's children, to the third and fourth generation. And Moses made haste to bow his head toward the earth and worshiped (Exodus 34:5-8 AMP).

As you can see, the people who did not enter into covenant with God and go up to the meeting place that God had designated on top of the mountain, really missed out on a tremendous relationship with the Lord.

We must be careful not to grieve the Holy Spirit Who has invited us into this wonderful communion with Him. We must learn to instantly obey His voice when He tells us to be alone on the mountain with God, or wherever the meeting place with God may be. We must recognize that our meeting place with God is of the Lord's choosing.

2. <u>Thunder, Lightning, Dense Cloud, and a Ram's Horn.</u>

"On the morning of the third day, thunder roared and lightning flashed, and a dense cloud came down on the mountain. There was a long, loud blast from a ram's horn, and all the people trembled. Moses led them out from the camp to meet with God, and they stood at the foot of the mountain. All of Mount Sinai was covered with smoke because the Lord had descended on it in the form of fire. The smoke billowed into the sky like smoke from a brick kiln, and the whole mountain shook violently. As the blast of the ram's horn grew louder and louder, Moses spoke, and God thundered his reply. The Lord came down on the top of Mount Sinai and called Moses to the top of the mountain. So Moses climbed the mountain (Exodus 19:16-20 NLT emphasis added)."

"The Lord came down on the top of Mount Sinai and called Moses to the top of the mountain" and here is the result:

- ❖ Thunder roared.
- ❖ Lightning flashed.
- ❖ A dense cloud came down on the mountain.
- ❖ A long, loud blast surrounded from a ram's horn.

❖ All the people trembled.

"Moses led them out (the people) from the camp to meet with God, and they stood at the foot of the mountain." Here is what they witnessed:

A. Mount Sinai was covered with smoke because the Lord had descended on it in the form of fire.

B. The smoke billowed into the sky like smoke from a brick kiln.

C. The whole mountain shook violently.

D. The blast of the ram's horn grew louder and louder.

E. Moses spoke, and God thundered.

3. **The Dark Cloud.**

"As the people stood in the distance, Moses approached **the dark cloud where God was** (Exodus 20:21 NLT emphasis added)."

The cloud of God can actually be so dense with His glory and presence that it will cloak (cover) Him. This is a mystery. When God appears, sometimes He hides Himself in the cloud. In science, we understand that matter can be so dense that light will not be able to escape the perimeter. Your eyes will not pick up the object. That is called a "black hole".

A "black hole" is a star (sun) that is so dense that light cannot escape from it because of the strong field that is around it. The element of that strong field helps us to understand what occurs in the presence of God and how His presence can become so intense that there are times on this earth when we cannot continue to work and to exist normally. This is a mystery of God.

> And it came to pass, when the priests came out of the Holy place, that the cloud filled the house of the Lord, so that the priests could not continue ministering because of the cloud; for the glory of the Lord filled the house of the Lord. Then Solomon spoke: "The Lord said He would dwell in the **dark cloud**. I have surely built You an exalted house, And a place for You to dwell in forever (1 Kings 8:10-13).

The power of God's anointing can cause someone to seemingly "freeze," or cause people to fall when the anointing touches them.

4. **The Glory of the Lord.**

> Then Moses climbed up the mountain, and the cloud covered it. And **the glory of the Lord settled down on Mount Sinai**, and the cloud covered it for six days. On the seventh day the Lord called to Moses from inside the cloud. To the Israelites at the foot of the mountain, **the glory of the Lord appeared at the summit like a consuming fire**. Then Moses disappeared **into the cloud** as he climbed higher up the mountain. He remained on the mountain forty days and forty nights (Exodus 24:15-18 NLT emphasis added).

The glory of the Lord can appear as an "All-Consuming Fire." The Lord can have this occur whenever He wants to reveal Himself that way. The cloud will not cloak Him, and the fire will appear and come forth. We should all desire "that same fire" as believers. We have been called to this Meeting Place on the mountain and our destiny will be revealed.

You should always yield to the fire. The fire will reveal that which is pure, that which is holy, and that which everlasting. After everything is consumed, which essentially means nothing is remaining, then the pure, the holy, and the everlasting will be revealed. You must go through the fire and you must be cleansed. The baptism of fire that John the Baptist talked about is different than being washed in the blood. The blood represents the positional work of Jesus Christ, Who has delivered us from our sins.

The Holy Fire is a purifying of the soul and the works of the flesh. God is a consuming fire. His desire is to work out all of the impurities of the carnal nature. Paul confronted the Corinthians with these carnal ways after they had become believers. These believers were still living in a carnal manner, according to Paul. Healing through the cleansing fire of God causes you to be transformed by the renewing of your mind by the Word of God.

HOLY CLEANSING FIRE

I remember right before September 11, 2001, when the Lord Jesus appeared to me and ministered to me about His holy cleansing fire. As in all of His appearances to me, there was nothing on my part that triggered the visit. I had been involved in a church in Phoenix, Arizona. It was the church my wife and I attended. At the time, I was being groomed for full- time ministry in the national organization to which the church belonged. As we worshipped in the service Sunday morning, I opened my eyes to see the worship leader and the choir worshipping the Lord. To my surprise, off to my right, was Jesus, standing beside the choir with His arms out in a receiving position, taking in our worship. You should have seen His face. He was in ecstasy as what we were doing that which pleased Him to the point of complete satisfaction!

I stopped and stared because He was so beautiful to watch. He looked to be of average height (just under six feet tall), with tanned skin and long brown hair with blonde highlights, which he parted down the middle. All of a sudden, He opened His eyes and knew that I was staring at Him. He seemed ignited as with a bright flame and was burning freely in front of everyone. At this point, I looked at the faces of all the people in the congregation to see their reaction to His appearance on the platform. Even my wife, who was beside me, did not see Him. I turned my attention back to the platform to behold the Master still burning. He was completely engulfed in flames from head to toe. I saw His right arm extend as He pointed directly at me! I noticed that a flaming stream was moving like lava away from Him and making its way off the platform and down the aisle toward me. My eyes had been opened by the Spirit, and I had all my faculties. He was just as clear to me as all the people that I saw around Him.

Soon, the flaming lava reached my feet and started up my legs. This felt so clean. It was amazing! It was His cleansing fire. I felt healing as it moved up to consume me. The whole time, I was hoping others could see the Lord Jesus in this most special appearance.

I was excited, because at this point, I realized I was about to get what Jesus had. The flames were about to be all over me. I was being set aflame in Jesus's name!

Then I became alarmed. Suddenly, as the flames got up past my waist, I began to experience extreme pain. As the flames proceeded up through my chest area, the pain became excruciating. I stopped worshipping and put my arms down and looked at Jesus with a look that asked, "What in the world is going on?" Immediately, without saying a word, Jesus showed me His mission, His intention.

I understood something about myself, as I burned. The area that the flames reached and were causing the pain was the area of my soul, which includes the mind, will, and emotions!

I was having trouble breathing. I knew if things did not change, I was in trouble. When I looked back at Jesus, His face got a very stern look on it as He spoke to me out loud. With a roar He proclaimed, "Yield to the fire!" When He said that, everything shook. I made an internal adjustment, by consciously yielding to the fire, and the pain suddenly stopped. The flames immediately went up over me and finished the cleansing work in me.

I realized afterward why I had gone through so many trials with so many people and situations in my life. I was being cleansed with Holy Fire!

Holy fire still burns today as I yield to what He is doing in my life. The flames will not go out because they are from Him. Yield to His work. Do not fight the process any more. This world does not deserve you after you have been put through the fire and have come out purified. It is as if you are pure gold without any impurities! You are beautiful, just as He is beautiful!

5. **The Lord was in the Cloud on the mountain.**

"Then **the Lord came down in a cloud** and stood there with him; and he called out his own name, Yahweh. The Lord passed in front of Moses, calling out,

Yahweh! The Lord!
The God of compassion and mercy!

I am slow to anger and filled with unfailing love and
faithfulness. I lavish unfailing love to a thousand generations.
I forgive iniquity, rebellion, and sin.
But I do not excuse the guilty. I lay the sins of the
parents upon their children and grandchildren;
the entire family is affected—
even children in the third and fourth generations.

Moses immediately threw himself to the ground and
worshipped. And he said, 'O Lord, if it is true that I
have found favor with you, then please travel with
us. Yes, this is a stubborn and rebellious people, but
please forgive our iniquity and our sins. Claim us as
your own special possession.' The Lord replied,
'Listen, I am making a covenant with you in the
presence of all your people. I will perform miracles
that have never been performed anywhere in all the
earth or in any nation. And all the people around you
will see the power of the Lord—the awesome power
I will display for you. But listen carefully to
everything I command you today (Exodus 34:4-11
NLT emphasis added).' "

YOUR APPOINTMENT

The Spirit of the Lord is calling all of us to the mountain of
God. We must not hesitate, but we must immediately accept
His invitation just as Moses did. The Lord loves it when you
do not hesitate and you are ready to act. There should never
be a time where you would not want to be in the Meeting
Place with God. He wants to be in covenant with you. As we
meet with Him, He will want to give the Kingdom to you (see
Luke 12:32). Wherever you find lack in your life, you will gain
what is an abundant supply through Him. That is because
when you make a covenant with the Lord, you get everything
that He has and He gets everything that you have.

Your whole future, your destiny, is about to be discussed

as you go to the Meeting Place with God. He desires that you ask Him the following items:

1) Ask Him to **teach** you His ways.
2) Ask Him to **show** you His Glory.
3) Ask Him to **baptize** you in Holy Fire.
4) Ask Him to **go with** you or you are not going.

"Don't miss your appointment with God on the mountain. He is waiting for you."

Chapter 4

The Tent Of Meeting / Tabernacle

$\mathcal{M}$oses took his tent and pitched it outside the camp, far from the camp, and called it the tabernacle of meeting. And it came to pass that everyone who sought the Lord went out to the tabernacle of meeting which was outside the camp. So it was, whenever Moses went out to the tabernacle, that all the people rose, and each man stood at his tent door and watched Moses until he had gone into the tabernacle. And it came to pass, when Moses entered the tabernacle, that the pillar of cloud descended and stood at the door of the tabernacle, and the Lord talked with Moses. All the people saw the pillar of cloud standing at the tabernacle door, and all the people rose and worshipped, each man in his tent door. So the Lord spoke to Moses face to face, as a man speaks to his friend. And he would return to the camp, but his servant Joshua the son of Nun, a young man, did not depart from the tabernacle (Exodus 33:7-11).

This special tent that Moses set up was for anyone who wanted to meet with the Lord. This shows the Lord's amazing mercy and grace toward His people. He provided a place to meet with Him, despite the people's rejection of Him. He did not give up, but he had Moses set up a tent where they could meet with Him.

It is amazing to me that no one is ever mentioned meeting with God except Moses and Joshua. This special place of meeting is highlighted here for an important reason. I believe that for those Christians who have not already responded to God's call to the mountain to be alone with Him, have been given another opportunity to meet with Him. The meeting place which God has provided is much more assessable to Him. That place can be reached easily, without the hindrance of others. It is a place to meet Him privately.

To summarize, all of this has been provided for your benefit. The amazing and wonderful things that happened because this tent of meeting has been built are to benefit you. It is important to note that many people do not seem to have taken advantage of this wonderful opportunity to meet with God. The fact that the people refused to meet with God in the tent must have hurt the Lord. And as we said before, they also had rejected His invitation to the mountain.

"Moses took his tent and pitched it outside the camp, far from the camp. He called it the tabernacle of meeting."

Seven Wonderful Facts About the Tent of Meeting

1.
Everyone who sought the Lord
went out to the tabernacle of meeting which was located outside the camp.

2.
When Moses entered the tabernacle,
then the pillar of cloud descended and stood at the door of the tabernacle.

3.
The Lord talked with Moses.

4.
All the people saw
the pillar of cloud standing at the tabernacle door.

5.
All the people rose and worshipped,
each man in his tent door.

6.
The Lord spoke to Moses face to face,
as a man speaks to his friend.

7.
His servant Joshua,
the son of Nun, a young man, did not depart from the tabernacle (see Exodus 33:7-11 emphasis added).

TWO PROFOUND EVENTS

1. The Lord Would Speak Face to Face with Moses.

This particular statement is one of the most profound pieces of information that I have ever read. Everyone talks about meeting with God, but very few have actually experienced a face-to-face conversation with Him. One significant quality that Moses possessed is that he learned not to hesitate when God spoke. When he was called up to the mountain to be with the Almighty, he obeyed quickly and the result was that a wonderful relationship with God was created.

If Moses was able to have such an intimate fellowship with the Lord, then how much more should we in this New Covenant be able to have a face-to-face encounter with the one who saved us from our sin? When God sets up a tent of meeting, be the first to respond to His call. He will reward you for your response by calling you a true friend of God.

2. The Cloud Covered and the Glory Filled.

Then the cloud covered the Tabernacle, and the glory of the Lord filled the Tabernacle. Moses could no longer enter the Tabernacle because the cloud had settled down over it, and the glory of the Lord filled the Tabernacle. Now whenever the cloud lifted from the Tabernacle, the people of Israel would set out on their journey, following it. But if the cloud did not rise, they remained where they were until it lifted. The cloud of the Lord hovered over the Tabernacle during the day, and at night fire glowed inside the cloud so the whole family of Israel could see it. This continued throughout all their journeys (Exodus 40:34-38 NLT emphasis added).

A. <u>The cloud covered the Tabernacle, and the glory of</u> <u>the Lord filled the Tabernacle.</u>*

Moses could no longer enter the Tabernacle because the cloud had settled down over it, and the glory of the Lord filled the Tabernacle.

This reveals what was given to us through Jesus Christ. The Holy Spirit was given to be upon us and in us, just as this tent, which was a tabernacle of meeting, was given to the children of Israel. We love when the Holy Spirit comes upon us in a tabernacle meeting. But remember, the greatest gift given us was the "in-filling" of the Holy Spirit on the Day of Pentecost. We must allow that glory to fill us to overflowing.

The relationship and closeness provided by the baptism of the Holy Spirit is a wonderful illustration of a meeting place with God. This meeting place makes it possible for God to satisfy your great desire for a full and intimate relationship with Him. Allow your meeting place with God to be so full of His glory that His anointing is not only upon you, but fully saturates your being. It should be such a potent saturation that no one near you can seem to function normally.

Supernatural manifestations of His glory should be the norm for the born-again, Spirit-filled believer. The Apostle Paul told us to, "... be filled with the Spirit, speaking to one another in psalms and hymns and spiritual songs, singing and making melody in your heart to the Lord (Ephesians 5:18-20)."

B. <u>Whenever the cloud lifted from the Tabernacle, the</u> <u>people of Israel would set out on their journey,</u> <u>following it.</u>*

The cloud lifting, with God's people responding and following, is a good example of how God leads and guides His children by the Holy Spirit. The Holy Spirit is not only within us, the Holy Spirit is also upon us. We must follow the glory cloud when God has us in transition.

It is comforting to know that we all have the Lord leading and guiding us. Be cognizant that when He is leading in a certain direction, He has your destiny and purpose at heart. He will never leave you nor forsake you (see Hebrews 13:5)!

C. But if the cloud did not rise, they remained where they were until it lifted.*

If the cloud stays where you are, then your meeting place with God remains the same. Even in the desert, God created this meeting place for His people. They were not allowed to move until the cloud did. So it is with us. God is with us wherever we are located, but we must also agree to follow Him where His presence leads us.

D. The cloud of the Lord hovered over the Tabernacle during the day.*

God hovers over us. When we are in this special meeting place with Him, we must realize that there are visible signs to others that we are abiding in Him and He in us (see John 15:4).

E. At night, fire glowed inside the cloud so the whole family of Israel could see it.*

I love the fire of God's Holy Spirit. It is a sign that He protects us, even in the dark hours of the night. The fire of His glory is burning bright and no enemy will come near you because of it. This was for a sign that God was with the children of Israel, and it is a sign that He is with us.

The fire glowing inside the cloud was a testimony for Israel to see that the Lord was watching over them. It was also a sign for the enemies of both God and Israel that God was watching over them. This sign can produce fear in the enemies of our soul.

God is with us as Christians. God's Holy Fire is part of the Holy Spirit's manifestation in our lives. The fire produces a cleansing and purification in our lives that cause us to desire to live holy, set apart lives.

Holy Fire is what John the Baptist mentioned concerning Jesus and His ministry. John said, "I indeed baptize you with water unto repentance, but He who is coming after me is mightier than I, whose sandals I am not worthy to carry. He will baptize you with the Holy Spirit and fire. His winnowing fan is in His hand, and He will thoroughly clean out His threshing floor, and gather His wheat into the barn; but He will burn up the chaff with unquenchable fire (Matthew 3:11-12)."

F. This continued throughout all their journeys.*

> Your God will be with for the whole journey through your desert experiences of testing and into your Promised Land of destiny and purpose. He is cultivating your relationship with Him as your faith grows and as you learn His ways.
> *(Exodus 40:34-38 NLT emphasis added).

Chapter 5

The Most Holy Place

The Lord, later through Moses, instituted the Ark of the Covenant. He instructed Moses to make an inner sanctuary called "The Most Holy Place." He had Moses build the Ark according to the specifications that the Lord had instructed Him on the "Mountain of God."

Now the Israelites move from the "Mountain of God" to a tabernacle or tent that will go with them in the desert. The "Ark of God" had the "Glory of God" Himself, hovering above the mercy seat in the cloud. God was having Moses set up a meeting place where God would meet with the high priest and there would be atonement for sins for all the people.

This place was set apart as "Most Holy". Only the High Priest could enter it as the book of Hebrews states, "... not that He should offer Himself often, as the high priest enters the Most Holy Place every year with blood of another (Hebrews 9:25 emphasis added)."

Jesus has shown me that when we pray in the Spirit, we are building ourselves up in our "Most Holy Faith" (see Jude 20). We do not always know how to pray, but the Spirit of God steps in on our behalf to assist and guide us. The Holy Spirit wants to help us pray into the Holy of Holies. When we will go there by faith to this special Meeting Place of God, by faith we are going to experience a deeply intimate time with the Lord. The Apostle Paul explains this to us in the book of Romans:

> And the Holy Spirit helps us in our weakness. For example, we don't know what God wants us to pray for. But the Holy Spirit prays for us with groanings that cannot be expressed in words. And the Father who knows all hearts knows what the Spirit is saying, for the Spirit pleads for us believers in harmony with God's own will. And we know that God causes everything to work together for the good of those who love God and are called according to his purpose for them. For God knew His people in advance, and He chose them to become like his Son, so that His Son would be the firstborn among many brothers and sisters. And having chosen them, He called them to come to Him. And having called them, He gave them right standing with Himself. And having given them right standing, He gave them His glory (Romans 8:26-31 NLT).

HOLY SPIRIT HELP

The Holy Spirit has been called alongside to help us in every area of our life. As we encounter the Holy Place of God, we find great intimacy with the Lord. This is a very special and exclusive meeting place with God.

If anyone can comprehend the extent of holiness, it would be the Holy Spirit. He takes that which is of God and gives it unto us, just as Jesus said. As the Holy Spirit takes us into this special meeting place with God, we need to first acknowledge that we need His help. Acknowledging that we need God's help is a form of true humility. He wants to help us in our weakness, but we must be humble and of a contrite heart so that He may dwell with us (see Isaiah 57:15).

After we have humbled ourselves before Him, He comes and dwells with us and helps us in our weaknesses. You see, sometimes we do not even have the understanding of what is going on in our own lives or even in the lives of others that may influence us. We find ourselves trying to reason out what God's will may be in situations, using our brains to troubleshoot problems. You know what I am talking about. We have all been there, at a point where we try to mentally assess what is happening rather than seek God's revelation about what is happening.

So in our journey to our Promised Land of destiny and purpose, we might not initially be aware of what God desires for us. We might not even know how to ask Him to explain, although we may have some understanding of the situation or the possibilities. That is why we must depend upon the Holy Spirit in this special meeting place. The Holy Spirit will teach us. He will instruct us and then pray through us. In that way, we will ask the Lord everything that God wants us to request, and we will pray the way He wants us to pray.

As we yield to the Spirit, we pray in an unknown language called "tongues". The Bible says that when we pray in this language, we are not understanding what we are saying in our own mind, we are praying directly to God with our spirit (see I Corinthians14:2).

Be aware that God, not only asked us to pray, but He has sent someone to help us. We might not understand what is coming out of our mouths; it might even just sound like groaning. That is because we do not have words in our own language to express what God is praying through our expressions.

**The Spirit will passionately plead for us
so that we will be in perfect harmony with Heaven and
all of the
plans of the Kingdom of God.**

One must remember that everything that is in your heart is known by the Father God. We need to have transparency toward God. Transparency will accelerate you in the Realms of God, especially in the Meeting Place with God.

Are you ready to allow the Holy Spirit to take hold of you in your weakness and begin to give you resurrection power in your prayers to Him? In this special meeting place, called the Most Holy Place, the Spirit of God is going to help you ask for the most important things. You will ask for these things in the most effective way.

The Holy Spirit is the best Intercessor we could ever have. He will be pleading on our behalf with groans that are too deep for words. The Spirit will ask, on our behalf, that we fulfill every Word that is written in heaven about us. He will help us fulfill what is recorded for us to do within our books that are located in the libraries of Heaven (see Psalms 139:16 NLT). The Spirit will passionately plead for us so that we will be in perfect harmony with Heaven and all of the plans of the Kingdom of God.

PURPOSE

God's plans for us are greater than our own (see Jeremiah 29:11). It is important to remember that His purpose will be fulfilled for those the that love God, and who are called according to His purpose.

God knew who His family would be long before we were born. Because of His infinite knowledge, He put together a plan for each one of us. His plan includes all of us being in a meeting place with God and the Spirit of God praying forth that plan. You see, the Spirit of God is actually just requesting something that was already given to you a long time ago, before the foundations of the earth.

You need to trust the Spirit of God. When you give Him access to your prayer life, He will ask for God's perfect plan every time. That plan will bring forth, wonderful, powerful, good things into our lives. Every detail of your life is before God, and He is bringing everything in His will for your life to pass, because we love Him and were designed to fulfill His purpose.

As we meet with Him it in this Most Holy Place, we realize that we were destined to share in the likeness of Jesus. His presence transforms us as we breathe in the atmosphere heaven.

CHOSEN

Think about it! He chose us to become like His Son, Jesus. He thought of us. He created this amazing plan, and as you are reading this now, you are fulfilling what has been all written down. It is written that you would come into the knowledge of who you are in Him. Your purpose and destiny are being revealed.

It is liberating to know that God chose you first, before you even knew Him. It is good also to know that He did all these good things for you in Christ without you earning any approval on your own. You see, God called us to Himself. We are set apart, chosen to be a Holy people, for His purpose alone.

CALLED

So now you know that God chose us in Him before the foundation of the world, He has now called you to draw close to Him. He wants you to come and stand with Him in the righteousness of God.

And having chosen us, He called us to come to Him. He wants you to stand with Him in the righteousness that Jesus bought for you. There is a righteous place for you to stand with Him. All you have to do is accept it by faith and make a conscious effort to come Him. Now you must meet with Him in the special place. Yield to the Spirit and answer the call to be in right-standing with Him. You will be forever changed in His presence.

RIGHT-STANDING

This right-standing with God is hard to comprehend because we find ourselves in situations where we do not fully believe what God has done for us. When we enter in to this Meeting Place with God, we may experience thoughts of rejection or inadequacy towards Him. We may have feelings of fear. Those are feelings that the enemy brings upon us. We must begin to realize that we are loved and accepted by Him. We have to learn to rest in His presence.

I am telling you the truth about who He is and what He has done for us. I decided to do this when I was sent back from Heaven in 1992. Everyone needs to know the Truth about Him. We have to realize this is what happened when God gave the Revelation that Paul, the Apostle, received and gave to us. In all the New Testament books that he wrote, he said, " If indeed you have heard of the dispensation of the grace of God which was given to me for you, how that by revelation He made known to me the mystery (as I have briefly written already, by which, when you read, you may understand my knowledge in the mystery of Christ), (Ephesians 3:2-5 emphasis added)."

It is good to see what has been obtained for us through Jesus Christ. Now, as we spend time in the Holy of Holies, we can come in with confidence, knowing that He has gone before us. The Holy Spirit has given us this revelation from the Word about right-standing in Christ. Now we can ask Him for anything and He will do it (see John 14:14).

GLORY

When we are in right standing with God and His presence fills us, we begin to realize that Jesus gave us the same glory that the Father gave to Him. This is what Jesus prayed about us in front of His disciples.

> "I am praying not only for these disciples but also for all who will ever believe in me through their message. I pray that they will all be one, just as you and I are one—as you are in me, Father, and I am in you. And may they be in us so that the world will believe you sent me. "I have given them the glory you gave me, so they may be one as we are one. I am in them and you are in me. May they experience such perfect unity that the world will know that you sent me and that you love them as much as you love me. Father, I want these whom you have given me to be with me where I am. Then they can see all the glory you gave me because you loved me even before the world began (John 17:20-24 NLT emphasis added)!

"I have given them the glory You gave me, so they may be one as We are one."
Jesus Christ

This is an exciting revelation. Jesus prayed for all of us who would believe. He stated that He has given us the same glory that was given to Him by the Father. Think about that for a few moments.

WE ARE ONE

"So that we may be one as He and the Father are one." This truth is so profound. When you are in the Holy of Holies with the Father, we are one with Him. We are His children. This is because of what Jesus Christ did for us after He rose from the dead. He ascended on high and was seated at the right hand of God. The Apostle Paul said, "What is the exceeding greatness of His power toward us who believe, according to the working of His mighty power which He worked in Christ when He raised Him from the dead and seated Him at His right hand in the heavenly places, far above all principality and power and might and dominion, and every name that is named, not only in this age but also in that which is to come (Ephesians 1:19-21 emphasis added)."

SEATED

There is always a great deal of conversation involving the death, burial, and resurrection of Christ to be found in religious circles. But the apostle Paul's teaching actually starts with the resurrection. It is a predominant theme. Paul continues by talking about being seated at the right hand of God. And some of us stop at the point where Jesus has been seated at the right hand of God, which is good in and of itself. However, the Apostle Paul's writings and revelations emphasize our present position with Jesus and God the Father. Paul said, "For He raised us from the dead along with Christ and seated us with Him in the heavenly realms because we are united with Christ Jesus. So God can point to us in all future ages as examples of the incredible wealth of his grace and kindness toward us, as shown in all he has done for us who are united with Christ Jesus (Ephesians 2:6-7 NLT emphasis added)."

ADOPTED

We have been adopted into the family of God. It is wonderful that we are seated with Him in the heavenly realms through Christ Jesus. We must also recognize the fact that we are His children. We are no longer servants or slaves, but heirs of God.

The Apostle Paul explained this when he said, "So you have not received a spirit that makes you fearful slaves. Instead, you received God's Spirit when He adopted you as His own children. Now we call Him, "Abba, Father." For His Spirit joins with our spirit to affirm that we are God's children. And since we are his children, we are his heirs. In fact, together with Christ we are heirs of God's glory. But if we are to share his glory, we must also share his suffering (Romans 8:15-17 NLT)."

It is important to recognize that Jesus went in to the Holy of Holies before us as the High Priest and offered His blood on our behalf. He has made a new and living way for us to be able to enter into the Holy of Holies.

Therefore, brethren, having boldness to enter the Holiest by the blood of Jesus, by a new and living way which He consecrated for us, through the veil, that is, His flesh, and having a High Priest over the house of God, let us draw near with a true heart in full assurance of faith, having our hearts sprinkled from an evil conscience and our bodies washed with pure water (Hebrews 10:19-22).

THE LORD IS PRESENT

Four Truths Concerning the Lord Is Present:

1. ### The Lord Himself is Present in the Cloud above the Ark.

   "The Lord said to Moses, 'Warn your brother, Aaron, not to enter the Most Holy Place behind the inner curtain whenever he chooses; if he does, he will die. For the Ark's cover—the place of atonement—is there, and I myself am present in the cloud above the atonement cover' (Leviticus 16:2 NLT emphasis added)."

2. ### The Cloud of Incense will Rise over the Ark.

   "Aaron will present his own bull as a sin offering to purify himself and his family, making them right with the Lord. After he has slaughtered the bull as a sin offering, he will fill an incense burner with burning coals from the altar that stands before the Lord. Then he will take two handfuls of fragrant powdered incense and will carry the burner and the incense behind the inner curtain. There in the Lord's presence he will put the incense on the burning coals so that a cloud of incense will rise over the Ark's cover—the place of atonement—that rests on the Ark of the Covenant. If he follows these instructions, he will not die. Then he must take some of the blood of the bull, dip his finger in it, and sprinkle it on the east side of the atonement cover. He must sprinkle blood seven times with his finger in front of the atonement cover (Leviticus 16:11-14 NLT emphasis added)."

3. ### There is a Regular Pattern of Cloud and Fire.

   "On the day the Tabernacle was set up, **the cloud covered it**. But from evening until morning **the cloud** over the Tabernacle looked like **a pillar of fire**. This was the regular pattern—at night the cloud that covered the Tabernacle had the **appearance of fire** (Numbers 9:15-17 emphasis added)."

4. **The Temple: A Place for God to Dwell.**

"When the priests came out of the Holy Place, **a thick cloud filled the Temple of the Lord**. The priests could not continue their service because of the cloud, for the glorious presence of the Lord filled the Temple. Then Solomon prayed, "O Lord, you have said that you would **live in a thick cloud of darkness**. Now I have built **a glorious Temple** for you, a place where you can live forever (1 Kings 8:10-13 NLT emphasis added)!"

Chapter 6

The Throne Room

*R*oyalty is associated with exquisite palaces, private wealth, luxurious amenities, power, honor, glory, and beauty. The facilities where royalty dwells is often a display beyond belief. It is hard to describe such quality when you have not encountered it previously.

Most of us dream of having a piece of jewelry with gold and precious stones. The homes of royalty often have floors, walls, and furniture made out of the same type of material that is used to create jewelry with precious metal and valuable gemstones. Royalty spares no expense. There are no limits. God's throne room is like this. We are called to meet with Him and worship Him in this special meeting place with God.

Remember that God is royalty.
He is breathtaking to behold. He is a King that sits on a
majestic throne, and rules from Eternity.
Yet, He knows my name and answers me
when I call.

BREATHTAKING

It takes a lot for me to have my breath taken away. I have seen so many beautiful things in my travels. I have experienced so many adrenaline-filled feats. I have experienced meeting the woman of my dreams and marrying her.

I have had angels come to visit me, causing me to be unable to stand any longer, while I have trembled at the Word of the Lord that they delivered to me. I have had the Lord Jesus Christ appear to me nineteen times and deliver many wonderful messages from His heart to mine. I have had the Holy Spirit come when I thought that I could not go on any longer, which was sometimes even daily, at my job.

I've endured unbearable, physical pain for years as I was believing God for healing. Suddenly, God supernaturally healed me. I have seen God perform supernatural debt cancellation, so that I had no debt left anywhere. Jesus came into our room and walked between my college roommate and me, changing both of us forever. Jesus announced that He had called me, and then He turned around and walked out.

But the **one thing** that I cannot get over, that takes my breath away every time I think of it, is when I looked into His eyes and saw that He remembered the day that He thought of me and spoke me into existence. I saw in His eyes that I had turned out just exactly the way that He wanted me to be, and He smiled at me.

That is what took my breath away. The fact that I was His idea, and not the idea of a man. He approved of me. He is the most majestic, awesome King I have ever met. And He takes my breath away every time. Why? Because He loves me enough to die for me so that I can be all that He purposed for me. He is a King and He left the realm of Heaven and all His divine attributes to become a man of no reputation to save me from eternal damnation in Hell.

That is why I Love Him so.
He left His throne to retrieve me and wash away my sin. He then invited me to sit beside Him in
Heaven at the right hand of God, to rule and reign with Him.
Forever.

Breathtaking and awesome is your power! So astounding and unbelievable is your might and strength when it goes on display! Your glorious throne rests on a foundation of righteousness and just verdicts. Grace and truth are the attendants who go before you. The happiest people on earth are those who worship you with songs. They firmly march along shouting with joy and shining in the radiance streaming from your face. We can do nothing but leap for joy all day long; for we know who you are and what you do, and you've exalted us on high. The glory of your splendor is our strength, and your marvelous favor makes us even stronger, lifting us even higher! You are our King, the Holiest One of all; your wrap-around presence is our protection(Psalm 89:13-18 TPT)!

HIS POWER

God's power is breathtaking. Because of His mercy, He does not show His anger now because of His Son's blood on the Mercy Seat. He is waiting for everyone to come to the knowledge of His son Jesus Christ. God has displayed His power in times past to His people and He will continue to do so. But there are certain displays of God's awesome power that are set in motion every day, such as the stars, the planets, the seasons, the oceans, and seed time and harvest. Even the birds do not labor, yet still, God takes care of them.

Our heart beats without us telling it to beat, and we take thousands of breaths a day without even thinking about it, even though He is the One who has given them to us. This is His power, and it is breathtaking. I tithe, and He rebukes the devourer for my sake. And, as if that is not great enough alone, He opens the windows of Heaven and pours out a blessing upon me that I can not contain (see Malachi 3:10).

I have witnessed the awesome grace of God in His preparation to set the destiny of our lives in place by actively orchestrating people's lives to convene together so we can fulfill His plans for the Kingdom of God. He is accomplishing it in a way that we are not always aware of His hand in our relationships with others. I have seen Him answer prayer, and that can be awesome. But it is even more awesome to me when He answers prayers that I have not yet uttered, even before I ask. He is an awesome God.

MIGHT AND STRENGTH

God is Mighty in all His ways. As He rules and reigns in eternity, He does not even age. He Is actually like a young man, even though He is called the Ancient of Days. He is so powerful, and yet He just waits for us to respond to His offer, the offer of His Son who makes our relationship with the Father possible. With His mighty arm, He worked salvation on this earth.

His mighty arm worked this salvation while sitting on

a throne. He has not aged a bit, nor is He even tired. That is how strong and Mighty our God is!

When His might and power goes on display, it is difficult to comprehend. He put His Son in a body and thereby worked such a great salvation on this earth, showing us how we should live in His Spirit. And then He allowed Himself to die on a cross in order to reconcile us all to God. He has displayed His strength to us and now He asks us to live in that strength each day with resurrection power.

That same resurrection power is the power that rose Jesus from the dead. That resurrection power displayed His might and power. It is beyond understanding that the same power that rose Jesus from the dead is dwelling in you and me. Mighty and powerful is our God. Thank you, Lord, for displaying Your power through the resurrection and seating us with You in the Heavenly realms.

GLORIOUS THRONE

Every king has a throne. It represents the seat of rule and power over his domain. Everything that the king stands for is the foundation of his kingdom and his ruling power. You will see his whole domain influenced by the foundation of his rule.

As God sits on His throne, He is King, There are layers under Him that make up the foundation of the throne. One layer is His righteousness and the other layer is His justice (see Psalm 89:14). God always does what is right in any given situation, He does not look away or turn a deaf ear when He realizes that something is not right.

When righteousness rules, justice will also rule.

Justice enforces righteousness. It is not good enough just to be right, you must also enforce what is right with justice. You must correct anything that does not line up perfectly with righteousness. God's throne is perfect; the foundation of His throne is perfect. Anything that God says is true, He will enforce truth when you ask Him not only for righteousness, but also for justice. He will come into the midst of your situation and bring justice because He stands for righteousness. All of the verdicts that He proclaims are enforced by His mighty angels. They will intervene and make things right in your life when you cry out to Him for justice.

ATTENDANTS

In a king's court, there are many attendants. These attendants are to minister to, and for, the king. They each have special assignments that help run the kingdom.

These mighty ministers in God's court are called angels. They are ministering spirits that are flames of fire and they harken unto His voice. They are always strengthened because they gain strength in His presence and by hearing His Word. As the Lord sits on His throne, Angels desire to do exactly what He tells them to do. Angels demonstrate God's grace throughout Heaven and on earth by representing Him and doing what His heart desires for people.

They also enforce God's truth. As ambassadors, they stand for who God is and make sure that the truth is known about God and His kingdom. These angels always go before Him and prepare the way so that God's will may be done as people cry out and humble themselves. He answers them with these angels as ministers of grace and truth. Because our angels stand before Him, we are always being represented before

God on His throne.

"So awesome are you, O Yahweh,
Lord God of Angel-Armies! Where could we find
anyone as glorious as you? Your faithfulness
shines all around you (Psalm 89:8 TPT)!"

HAPPY PEOPLE

Psalms 89:15 says that the "happiest people on the earth or ones who worship" the One who sits on the throne with songs. The Apostle Paul talks about this in his writings (see Ephesians 5:19).

People who worship the King on the throne are putting their trust in His domain of power, trusting He Who sits on the throne. They are full of joy. God is full of glory, and His radiance shines out from His face and encompasses those who worship Him. When you worship, God's glory will affect you. When God smiles, glory streams from Him and comes to you. The glory of God strengthens you and fills you with joy. It will make you want to jump and shout.

Listed below are eight things to meditate on at the end of Psalms 89:15. These items describe our God, the One who sits on His throne. As you meditate on these things, remember that this is a special meeting place with God in which He rules not only the whole universe, but your life as well.

Nine Things to Meditate on Concerning the One Who Sits on the Throne Before His People:

1. We can do nothing but leap for joy all day long.*
2. We know Who You are and what You do.*
3. You have exalted us on high.*
4. The glory of Your splendor is our strength.*

5. Your marvelous favor makes us even stronger.*
6. It lifts us even higher!*
7. You are our King.*
8. You are the Holiest One of all.*
9. Your wrap-around presence is our protection.*
   *(see Psalm 89:16-18 TPT)!

I SAW THE LORD

What I am about to say may seem over-simplified Because I have experienced the joy of actually being before the Lord of Heaven on various occasions, I know that most of our problems would virtually disappear if we would allow the reality of the Throne Room to be ever before us. May God intervene in your life by giving you this reality that is written in the Word of God, the reality of knowing that His Holy Presence is with you always. His Holy Presence is what many Christians have experienced in this awesome meeting place with God.

Those who genuinely have experienced the Throne Room have a residue of the great anointing from that place. In the Throne Room, there is a noticeable level of God's awesome presence in the lives of those who have been transformed by revelation. I was compelled to read the Word of God after I had experienced His presence in the Throne Room.

ISAIAH

The prophet Isaiah was a privileged person because he observed the environment of the Throne Room. He proclaimed, "Yet I have seen the King, the Lord of Heaven's Armies (Isaiah 6:5)." This is an awesome sight to behold I will never forget the day that I saw the Throne Room of God myself.

Once you see the Lord, you will realize that you really did not know anything about Him except what you read. Once you actually find yourself standing before Him, His will becomes much more of a reality in your life. We often fail to allow the Spirit of God to make the Words of the Bible come alive and paint the proper multidimensional portrait of the realms of God that are found within His precious Word.

I venture to say that as you are reading this, you probably know you need to repent. As I recall some of the wonderful things that God has permitted me to see, I want to repent. I find myself repenting all the time, even though I am aware I am always in the position of righteousness with God. It is my relationship with Him that needs to grow in trust. It needs to grow by faith, not by sight. We must develop our ability to have faith in God before seeing what He has done. We must walk by faith, not by sight.

When I see Him, God is always so much more than I imagine, I realize that I need to allow the Holy Spirit to paint my world. His perspective is the viewpoint that we need to have to see things as God desires we see them. This acknowledgment helps me to receive what God speaks and know His Word is truth. It helps me to attain the place where I can meet Him, the place where He is not diminished and I am lifted up to where He is found.

I hesitate to tell you some of the things I have seen. I am not permitted to tell you everything. I do want to recall one engagement that I had in the Throne Room. I did not know that I had a scheduled appointment to be with the Lord there, but He had decided to show this to me. It was a big surprise when I was in prayer and found myself in the Throne Room.

On the day that this encounter happened, I want to emphasize that I had not been more well-behaved or fasting. We were not doing any thing out of the ordinary that day. My wife and I pray often. We miss meals here and there. But I do not think any of these things were a factor contributing to my finding myself in the Throne Room on that day.

I found myself looking out at the multitudes in white robes singing one song in one unified voice. I was not permitted to bring the song back, but I believe it was the song of the redeemed. The multitudes I observed may have been saints, angels, or both. They were as far as I could see. They were worshipping the One Who sits on the Throne. All of a sudden, I became troubled because I was actually sitting at the right hand of Jesus on a small throne.

The apostle Paul talked about this very situation in the book of Ephesians and Colossians. He said we are seated with Him in the heavenly realms (see Ephesians 2:6). It was overwhelming to realize that I was with Jesus, looking out over the multitudes. In the book of Revelation, John quoted Jesus that those who are overcomers will sit on the throne with Jesus. I knew that this was an accurate and scriptural situation.

However, being seated on that throne at the right hand of Jesus was still uncomfortable for me at the time. I turned to the left to look at Jesus. He was basking in the worship of the saints as they sang the song of the redeemed about the precious Lamb that was slain. Jesus did not look at me initially because He was receiving the worship in high praise of the multitudes of those before the throne.

I leaned forward again. I saw that everyone was giving themselves over to worship in the Throne Room. I started to slide out of the small throne. I was just going to slip down quietly to the front row and turn around and worship with my fellow servants, angels, and the saints who have gone before me.

All of a sudden, Jesus looked at me and stopped me before I could get my feet to the ground. He said, "This seat is for you. You can come here anytime you wish in prayer and sit with me. Come sit here as long as you like. Stay until you get your answer, and then take it back with you. You see, at my throne there are no questions, just answers. Get your answer, and take it back with you."

Then, I was quickly ushered back to my home. I continued on with what I was doing at that time. I do not know if I was in the body or out of the body. This experience changed my life forever because I now know that the Lord is so celebrated in such a way at all times. While here on the earth, we do not seek to have that reality. There are times that we go astray and we think that we cannot trust Him. The world seems to have an influence over us at certain times, and that seems to diminish our connection with Jesus. Everything seems to be going well, and then you meet Him face-to-face. You realize that you did not see, hear, or experience much of what He has for you. Who Jesus is as a Person becomes such a reality that you see your great need to repent. This experience causes you to desire to go to another level with Him in your walk of faith.

This is what happened to Isaiah the prophet. He realized that he was undone in the presence of God. Heaven's Throne Room has higher standards than we can fathom unless the Holy Spirit gives us the complete revelation when He takes us there Himself. Here is what the Prophet Isaiah encountered:

It was in the year King Uzziah died that I saw the Lord. He was sitting on a lofty throne, and the train of his robe filled the Temple. Attending him were mighty seraphim, each having six wings. With two wings they covered their faces, with two they covered their feet, and with two they flew. They were calling out to each other,

"Holy, Holy, Holy is the Lord of Heaven's Armies! The whole earth is filled with his glory!"

71

Their voices shook the Temple to its foundations, and the entire building was filled with smoke. Then I said, "It's all over! I am doomed, for I am a sinful man. I have filthy lips, and I live among a people with filthy lips. Yet I have seen the King, the Lord of Heaven's Armies." Then one of the seraphim flew to me with a burning coal he had taken from the altar with a pair of tongs. He touched my lips with it and said, "See, this coal has touched your lips. Now your guilt is removed, and your sins are forgiven (Isaiah 6:1-7 NLT)!

EZEKIEL

The prophet Ezekiel was told that God's throne would be placed in the midst God's people, the children of Israel. This is an amazing statement. It reminds me of the many Bible verses that talk about an eternal throne, especially in scriptures concerning king David and the country of Israel. Isaiah confirms Ezekiel's revelation by saying, "Of the increase of His government and peace There will be no end, upon the throne of David and over His kingdom, to order it and establish it with judgment and justice from that time forward, even forever. The zeal of the Lord of hosts will perform this (Isaiah 9:7)."

The Lord is protective and jealous over the things that He claims as His own. He puts His throne wherever He wants to place it and starts reigning. I want to be where He is! This throne is a special seat of power and authority. He has invited us to come to His throne and meet with Him. "Let us therefore come boldly to the throne of grace, that we may obtain mercy and find grace to help in time of need (Hebrews 4:16)."

Then I heard Him speaking to me from the temple, while a man stood beside me. And He said to me, "Son of man, this is the place of My throne and the place of the soles of My feet, where I will dwell in the midst of the children of Israel forever (Ezekiel 43:6-7).

This is exciting! The Lord wants to come to a place where He can be in the midst of His children. The very soles of His feet are going to touch the land of Israel. I believe that His throne is in the midst of the church, the body of Jesus Christ. I believe that He dwells among His people in the new covenant. Every time that we can get together as children of God, we present ourselves before the throne of God. We should do it. This is an amazing Meeting Place with God. We enter the throne room in the midst of His people through our worship.

DANIEL

The prophet Daniel also saw the throne of God. He witnessed all of the activity in the throne room. Daniel was overcome by the recollection of his visit to the throne room of God.

"I watched till thrones were put in place,
And the Ancient of Days was seated;
His garment was white as snow,
And the hair of His head was like pure wool.
His throne was a fiery flame,
Its wheels a burning fire;
A fiery stream issued
And came forth from before Him.
A thousand thousands ministered to Him;
Ten thousand times ten thousand stood before Him.
The court was seated,
And the books were opened (Daniel 7:9-10 TPT).

Ten Things to Meditate on Concerning the One Who Sits on the Throne and His Attendants

1. The Ancient of Days was seated.*

The Ancient of Days is our Heavenly Father Who has never aged as we age in this fallen realm called earth. He is actually a young man who never aged. If we were destined to live on this earth without ever aging, we would never see death.

From our standpoint, the truth that He is ancient is because He is not bound by time or space. The spirit realm has no boundaries as we do on the earth. It may be difficult for us to think that God could always exist and live forever. When I was with Him, I realized that it was impossible not to understand that God always existed. However, I came to realize that when we try to comprehend God in our flesh, our own understanding will never be enlightened unless the Spirit of God reveals this truth to us. He is eternal. He is seated in a restful, peaceful, confident place called His throne.

2. His garment was white as snow.*

His garments are beyond description because they are completely full of light and life. They are created with substance that is not available in the earth realm unless it is sent from heaven to earth in a visitation of the Spirit of God. God is so pure and holy that if it were not for the blood of Jesus, we would never be able to know Him in this way. He is far beyond beautiful. He is wonderful, glorious, majestic, and matchless.

3. And the hair of His head was like pure wool.*

Even His hair is pure and holy. It appears to be completely pure and clean. He is glorious to behold when we seek Him and look upon Him in this Meeting Place. We receive His glory into us. His glory comes by the washing of the water the Word and by the hope that we have. We have been redeemed by the blood of the Lamb, and we are called His children. "Beloved, now we are children of God; and it has not yet been revealed what we shall be, but we know that when He is revealed, we shall be like Him, for we shall see Him as He is. And everyone who has this hope in Him purifies himself, just as He is pure (1 John 3:2-4)."

4. His throne was a fiery flame.*

One of the attributes of God that is my favorite is the flame of Holy Fire that His presence and glory produce everywhere He goes. He is so holy that the space around Him becomes fire as it continually purifies His environment.

There is an awesome trembling that goes on before the throne. It is the fear of the Lord, and He is awesome. King David spoke of this in Psalm 19:9. "The fear of the Lord is clean, enduring forever; the judgments of the Lord are true and righteous altogether."

5. Its wheels a burning fire.*

These wheels are mentioned by Daniel. They are not explained or described, except that they are "burning fire!" However, Ezekiel also saw them in a heavenly visitation and recorded a more descriptive account. Ezekiel recounts, "As for the likeness of the living creatures, their appearance was like burning coals of fire, like the appearance of torches going back and forth among the living creatures. The fire was bright, and out of the fire went lightning. And the living creatures ran back and forth, in appearance like a flash of lightning. Now as I looked at the living creatures, behold, a wheel was on the earth beside each living creature with its four faces. The appearance of the wheels and their workings was like the color of beryl, and all four had the same likeness. The appearance of their workings was, as it were, a wheel in the middle of a wheel (Ezekiel 1:13-17)."

6. A fiery stream issued and came forth from before Him.*

I know that most of us know about the River of Life that flows from the throne of God, but did you know that there is also a fiery stream as well coming from God Himself? The prophet Isaiah saw God's breath as a stream of brimstone that burns:

The breath of the Lord, like fire from a volcano,

will set it ablaze

(Isaiah 30:33 NLT).

7. A thousand thousands ministered to Him.*

"Are they not all ministering spirits sent forth to minister for those who will inherit salvation (Hebrews 1:14 emphasis added)?"

8. Ten thousand times ten thousand stood before Him.*

"Now Enoch, the seventh from Adam, prophesied about these men also, saying, 'Behold, the Lord comes with ten thousands of His saints,' to execute judgment on all, to convict all who are ungodly among them of all their ungodly deeds which they have committed in an ungodly way, and of all the harsh things which ungodly sinners have spoken against Him (Jude 14-15 emphasis added)."

9. The court was seated.*

"But the court shall be seated,

And they shall take away his (Anti-Christ) dominion,

To consume and destroy it forever.

Then the kingdom and dominion,
and the greatness of the kingdoms under the whole heaven,
shall be given to the people, the saints of the Most High.
His kingdom is an everlasting kingdom,
And all dominions shall serve and obey Him
(Daniel 7:26-27 NLT)."

10. The books were opened.*

"You saw me before I was born.
Every day of my life was recorded in your book.
Every moment was laid out
before a single day had passed (Psalms 139:16 NLT
emphasis added)."

"Yet now, if You will forgive their sin — but if not, I pray, blot
me out of Your book which You have written (Exodus 32:32
emphasis added)."

"Therefore it is said in the Book of the Wars of the Lord
(Numbers 21:14 emphasis added)."

"Then those who feared the Lord spoke to one another,
And the Lord listened and heard them;
So a book of remembrance was written before Him
For those who fear the Lord
And who meditate on His name
(Malachi 3:16 emphasis added)."

"And I saw the dead, small and great, standing before God,
and books were opened. And another book was opened,
which is the Book of Life. And the dead were judged
according to their works, by the things which were written in
the books (Revelation 20:12-13 emphasis added)."

*(see Daniel 7:9-10 TPT)

FATHER GOD'S TESTIMONY

" 'The Lord said to my Lord,
'Sit at My right hand,
Till I make Your enemies Your footstool.'

Therefore let all the house of Israel know assuredly that God has made this Jesus, whom you crucified, both Lord and Christ (Acts 2:34-36 emphasis added)."

"The Lord said to my Lord,
'Sit at My right hand,
Till I make Your enemies Your footstool.'
The Lord shall send the rod of Your strength out of Zion.
Rule in the midst of Your enemies (Psalm 110:1-2 emphasis added)!"

"But to the Son He (God the Father) says: 'Your throne, O God, is forever and ever; a scepter of righteousness is the scepter of Your kingdom. You have loved righteousness and hated lawlessness; therefore God, Your God, has anointed You with the oil of gladness more than Your companions.' And: 'You, Lord, in the beginning laid the foundation of the earth, and the heavens are the work of Your hands. They will perish, but You remain; And they will all grow old like a garment; like a cloak You will fold them up, and they will be changed. But You are the same, and Your years will not fail (Hebrews 1:8-12 emphasis added)!' "

"Now this is the main point of the things we are saying: We have such a High Priest, who is seated at the right hand of the throne of the Majesty in the heavens, a Minister of the sanctuary and of the true tabernacle which the Lord erected, and not man (Hebrews 8:1-2 emphasis added)."

JOHN

Immediately I was in the Spirit; and behold, a throne set in heaven, and One sat on the throne. And He who sat there was like a jasper and a sardius stone in appearance; and there was a rainbow around the throne, in appearance like an emerald. Around the throne were twenty-four thrones, and on the thrones I saw twenty-four elders sitting, clothed in white robes; and they had crowns of gold on their heads. And from the throne proceeded lightnings, thunderings, and voices. Seven lamps of fire were burning before the throne, which are the seven Spirits of God. Before the throne there was a sea of glass, like crystal. And in the midst of the throne, and around the throne, were four living creatures full of eyes in front and in back. The first living creature was like a lion, the second living creature like a calf, the third living creature had a face like a man, and the fourth living creature was like a flying eagle. The four living creatures, each having six wings, were full of eyes around and within. And they do not rest day or night, saying:

"Holy, holy, holy,
Lord God Almighty,
Who was and is and is to come!"

Whenever the living creatures give glory and honor and thanks to Him who sits on the throne, who lives forever and ever, the twenty-four elders fall down before Him who sits on the throne and worship Him who lives forever and ever, and cast their crowns before the throne, saying:

"You are worthy, O Lord,
To receive glory and honor and power;
For You created all things, And by Your will
They exist and were created (Revelation 4:2-11 emphasis added)."

And I looked, and behold, in the midst of the throne and of the four living creatures, and in the midst of the elders, stood a Lamb as though it had been slain, having seven horns and seven eyes, which are the seven Spirits of God sent out into all the earth. Then He came and took the scroll out of the right hand of Him who sat on the throne. Now when He had taken the scroll, the four living creatures and the twenty-four elders fell down before the Lamb, each having a harp, and golden bowls full of incense, which are the prayers of the saints. And they sang a new song, saying:

"You are worthy to take the scroll,
And to open its seals;
For You were slain,
And have redeemed us to God by Your blood
Out of every tribe and tongue and people and nation,
And have made us kings and priests to our God;
And we shall reign on the earth."

Then I looked, and I heard the voice of many angels around the throne, the living creatures, and the elders; and the number of them was ten thousand times ten thousand, and thousands of thousands, saying with a loud voice:

"Worthy is the Lamb who was slain
To receive power and riches and wisdom,
And strength and honor and glory and blessing
(Revelation 5:6-12 emphasis added)!"

Chapter 7

The Secret Place

One thing I have desired of the Lord, that will I
seek: That I may dwell in the house of the
Lord all the days of my life, to behold the
beauty of the Lord, and to inquire in His
temple. For in the time of trouble He shall
hide me in His pavilion; in the secret place of
His tabernacle He shall hide me; He shall set
me high upon a rock. And now my head shall
be lifted up above my enemies all around me;
Therefore I will offer sacrifices of joy in His
tabernacle; I will sing, yes, I will sing praises
to the Lord (Psalm 27:4-6 emphasis added).

ONE THING

King David sought one thing above everything else. That
one thing, he said was "above all else" and was something
"I crave" (see Psalm 27:4 TPT). What was it? It was the
Secret Place; the special Meeting Place with God. He
desired to have God with him all the time. He desired it so

much that He wanted to go live with God in His House! He wanted to behold His face and enjoy Him in all of His beauty.

Can you imagine with me what that would be like? You would say, "He is awesome as He takes your breath away." You can just take Him in all day as you see His glory and encounter His grace.

While in His house, you would immediately realize that you should begin to offer up prayers. You are already in the Secret Place. As you pray, He hears you and is excited to answer your prayers because you are so close to Him.

When you have trouble, you will already have a safe place to hide as you seek refuge in His arms of Love. He is so strong and holy. The enemy would not even dare to approach the door.

SAFE

You are kept safe and protected in the security of His dwelling. You have made the Most High my dwelling place (see Psalm 91:9). You will be triumphant in everything you do because you stay in the Secret Place of the Lord. I will always be certain to offer Him praise and adoration. I never hold back from Him. I can experience the overflowing joy of being with Him.

How exciting is it to have a genuine relationship with the Almighty. The Lord has invited you in, and it is time to shout!

Yes, listen and you can hear the fanfare of my shouts of praise to the Lord! (Psalm 27: 6 TPT emphasis added).

HIDDEN

One of the advantages of being in the Secret Place, is that you are hidden in His presence. This keeps you safe from any evil plan of man that is against you. The secret place will protect you from every evil act or word. You will be so caught up in His presence that you will not hear what man is saying. You will not even know about these plans because you dwell with the Most High!

**You shall hide them in the
secret place of Your presence from the plots of man;
You shall keep them secretly in a pavilion from
the strife of tongues
(Psalm 31:20 emphasis added).**

Meeting God face-to-face in the secret place will deliver you from the fear of man. King Solomon gave us good advice when he said, "The fear of man brings a snare, but whoever trusts in the Lord shall be safe (Proverb 29:25)."

You always need to remember that your reward is with the Lord. You have been privileged to live with Him in this Secret Place, so you must realize that you do not need to try to impress man. Nothing else matters except pleasing Him. Just go and pray in the Secret Place, and you will get your answer publically without saying a word to anyone else.

Even Jesus Himself recommended this when He taught. "But you, when you pray, go into your room, and when you have shut your door, pray to your Father who is in the secret place; and your Father who sees in secret will reward you openly (Matthew 6:6 emphasis added)."

**When you sit enthroned under
the shadow of Shaddai, you are hidden in the strength
of God Most High. He's the hope that holds me, and the
Stronghold to shelter me, the only God for me,
and my great Confidence (Psalms 91:1,2 TPT).**

Chapter 8

The Glory and Covenant of Jesus

THE ULTIMATE MEETING PLACE

*W*hen the Godhead had decided that it was the optimal moment, Jesus was sent by the Holy Spirit into Mary's womb. He grew up and learned the ways of mankind. After being proven in the desert, Jesus came out in the power of the Holy Spirit and ministered to the people in very profound ways. Healing and deliverance was brought forth with great power as He destroyed the works of the devil.

Many put their trust in Him as soon as the people discerned that He was the Messiah This was predominantly based on all the signs and wonders the followed Him.

Others, were not so sure. They questioned if He truly was the one that was to come.

Eventually Jesus began to speak about His Father who sent Him to do the work of the Father and speak the words of the Father. Because Jesus claimed that God was His Father, the Jewish religious leaders became offended. Great controversy arose because those religious leaders knew they could lose control over the people. The glory had departed from the temple many years previous to that time, but they had not told anyone. The veil was still in place, but the presence was gone.

One day Jesus chose three disciples to come up to the mountain to have a private meeting with Him. Those three disciples did not know that they were about to witness an amazing display of glory. They were to have a very special meeting with God. Jesus knew that was what they would experience. Jesus will also do this for you: He will prepare a special Meeting Place with God just for you.

Even the disciples questioned the authenticity and origin of the works that Jesus performed. They saw the controversy that surrounded Him, and at times, they did not know whether to accept what Jesus did and said. Because the disciples did have doubts about the authenticity and origin of Jesus's power. Jesus chose to reveal His preexistence with the Father in the fulfillment of the law and the prophets in one visitation. It was done in one special meeting place with God. The revelation of His transfiguration showed that He was the fulfillment of the law and the prophets. It confirms that we are to see Him as the Son of God, and Him alone.

Then Jesus confirmed to everyone that we will someday see Jesus coming back in full glory and power. He said when you see the signs of the times happening, look up for your deliverance is near.

Later, to confirm this, Jesus was taken up in the cloud. Those who were with Him saw Him rising to Heaven. The angels were standing by and told the men who were with Him that He will return in the same way on the same glory cloud as He left . Those present could not see Him anymore, but they were told He would come back.

And finally, the Apostle John saw the Son of Man seated on the cloud with a golden crown on His head and a sharp sickle in His hand, ready to harvest and implement the Age to come because it was time.

These are all special meeting times with God. They come through our Lord Jesus Christ. He is full of glory, He has a glory cloud that envelopes Him. He is coming back soon on a glory cloud. Jesus has been designated as the center of the Meeting Place with God.

Four Important Meeting Places With Jesus and His Cloud of Glory

A. **A Bright Cloud of Glory.** "But even as He spoke, **a bright cloud** came over them, and a voice from the cloud said, 'This is my dearly loved Son, who brings me great joy. Listen to him.' The disciples were terrified and fell face down on the ground. Then Jesus came over and touched them. 'Get up,' he said. 'Don't be afraid.' And when they looked, **they saw only Jesus** (Matthew 17:5-8 NLT emphasis added)."

B. **Jesus was Taken up in the Cloud.** "After saying this, he was **taken up into a cloud** while they were watching, and they could no longer see him. As they strained to see Him rising into heaven, two white-robed men suddenly stood among them. 'Men of Galilee,' they said, 'Why are you standing here staring into heaven? Jesus has been taken from you into heaven, but someday he will return from heaven in the same way you saw him go' (Acts 1:9-11 NLT emphasis added)!"

C. **Jesus will Return on the Cloud.** "Then everyone will see **the Son of Man coming on a cloud with power and great glory.** So when all these things begin to happen, stand and look up, for your salvation is near (Luke 21:27-28 NLT emphasis added)!"

D. **Jesus was Seated on the Cloud.** "Then I saw a **white cloud**, and seated on the cloud was someone like **the Son of Man.** He had a gold crown on his head and a sharp sickle in his hand (Revelation 14:14 NLT emphasis added)."

COMMUNION

**Therefore, my beloved,
flee from idolatry. I speak as to wise men;
judge for yourselves what I say. The cup of blessing
which we bless, is it not the communion of the blood of
Christ? The bread which we break, is it not the
communion of the body of Christ? For we, though
many, are one bread and one body;
for we all partake of that
one bread
(1 Corinthians 10:14-17).**

One of the most powerful meeting places that God has made available to us in the New Covenant is communion. There is nothing greater that God has done for us than making a binding agreement called the "Covenant of the Blood". The apostle Paul taught us in his letter to the Corinthian Church, "For I received from the Lord that which I also delivered to you: that the Lord Jesus on the same night in which He was betrayed took bread; and when He had given thanks, He broke it and said, 'Take, eat; this is My body which is broken for you; do this in remembrance of Me.' In the same manner He also took the cup after supper, saying, 'This cup is the new covenant in My blood. This do, as often as you drink it, in remembrance of Me.' For as often as you eat this bread and drink this cup, you proclaim the Lord's death till He comes (1 Corinthians 11:23-26 emphasis added)."

This is a sacred time to honor Jesus for His sacrifice for you on the cross. This event occurred long before you were born. When we honor Him with our worship during this sacred observance, He will confirm His covenant with you as He promised (see Psalm 89:33-37).

Jesus graciously explained the spiritual dynamics of communion to us and the disciple, John, recorded it. After studying this particular passage, we will discuss what is happening in the spirit realm when you choose to come to God the Father and observe communion in this beautiful meeting place with God!

> "I tell you the truth, anyone who believes has eternal life. Yes, I am the bread of life! Your ancestors ate manna in the wilderness, but they all died. Anyone who eats the bread from heaven, however, will never die. I am the living bread that came down from heaven. Anyone who eats this bread will live forever; and this bread, which I will offer so the world may live, is

my flesh." Then the people began arguing with each other about what he meant. "How can this man give us his flesh to eat?" they asked. So Jesus said again, "I tell you the truth, unless you eat the flesh of the Son of Man and drink his blood, you cannot have eternal life within you. But anyone who eats my flesh and drinks my blood has eternal life, and I will raise that person at the last day. For my flesh is true food, and my blood is true drink. Anyone who eats my flesh and drinks my blood remains in me, and I in him. I live because of the living Father who sent me; in the same way, anyone who feeds on me will live because of me. I am the true bread that came down from heaven. Anyone who eats this bread will not die as your ancestors did (even though they ate the manna), but will live forever (John 6:47-58 emphasis added)."

BELIEVING IN JESUS

He is Living Reality.

Jesus is the epitome of "Living Reality." When Jesus speaks, His words are true, and life springs out from His words. Anything Jesus says to you is something He is able to fulfill in your life. That is why, through communion, we need to unite our hearts with His in an observance of the sacred covenant that we have with Him and Father God. When we unite with Him in communion, we are acknowledging the covenant that brings us eternal life. All we have to do is simply allow our hearts to connect and believe that He is the chosen sacrificial Lamb that was slain.

He is the Bread of Life.

Jesus referred to Himself as the Bread of Life. He

reminded the people that the manna that came down from heaven and fed their ancestors in the desert, represented a miracle for them. Despite this miraculous provision, they all still died.

Your ancestors ate manna in the desert and died. When you eat of the true bread that comes from Heaven, through communion with Him, He promised that you will never die. Jesus stood before them and presented Himself as the new Manna, the true Bread from Heaven.

He is Living Bread from Heaven.

So we have established that Jesus is the Bread of Life. He is food from Heaven for eternity. He will never cease, and you will never cease. You will live forever. This is very important to acknowledge when you meet with God at the communion table. Time is no longer a factor in your relationship with Jesus because He will feed you of Himself so that you can live forever, just as He lives forever. He has given His body as a sacrifice for you. He did this as a gift so that you may live forever. You can live eternally because Jesus thought you were worth paying the price that He had to pay!

He is Eternal Life.

Here is where Jesus revealed something that was very difficult for the people to accept. He told them that the only way that they could have eternal life was to eat the body of the Son of Man and drink His blood. If you recall, they had to kill and eat the sacrificial lamb on Passover in order to be protected from the angel of death.

He promises that those who do this will be raised up on the last day, in the resurrection. Jesus revealed that He wants us to eat and take all of Him into our being. That is why the observance of communion is a very special meeting place with God.

He is Real Spiritual Food

Jesus reveals to us that He is real spiritual food for your spirit man. So when you partake of the Bread of Life, which represents Jesus' body, you are receiving real food that will cause your spirit to flourish, no matter what this the environment that you may find yourself encountering on the earth may be. He also states that His blood is "real drink".

This is hard to an understand. It is stated in the Old Testament, by Moses, that we should, "Never eat the blood, for the blood is the life, and you must not eat the lifeblood with the meat. Instead, pour out the blood on the ground like water. Do not eat the blood, so that all may go well with you and your children after you, because you will be doing what pleases the Lord (Deuteronomy 12:23-25 NLT emphasis added)."

He who Partakes of Jesus Becomes One with Him.

Jesus clearly explains how important it is to become one with Him. During this Meeting Place experience with Jesus, you partake of Him and He will live in you in a profound way. This is not fantasy, this is reality. Jesus will become part of you as you partake of Him. He will live His life in you and through you.

The Father of Life Sent Him.

Remember that Jesus originated in Heaven. It was God the Father's plan to send Him as a Sacrificial Lamb for humanity. So God the Father sent you life from Heaven. I want you to partake of the spiritual food of Jesus's body and His blood. Remember the Father sent Him to give you life. His name is Jesus.

He Will Become Your Life if You Feed on Him.

The Lord has a plan for you this day. Part of discovering your destiny is based on the revelation that the Spirit gives you about God's kingdom and His plan. If you will faithfully feed on Jesus everyday, He will become your life. The Spirit will take that which is of Jesus and provide revelation of Him to you. Your destiny is unfolding, and you are becoming more like Him. Remember, you will live forever through Jesus Christ.

"Eat this Bread and you will live forever!"
John 6:58 TPT

Chapter 9

The Outpouring of the Holy Spirit

After Jesus left the earth in His ascension, the people seemed to have forgotten what Jesus said about the coming Holy Spirit. He was the Comforter, Who was to be just like Him and carry on Jesus's ministry on the earth through His disciples and the believers that would come after them. At times, they were just as shortsighted as we sometimes can be.

Because they did not know the big picture about God's plan for His kingdom on earth, they thought that Jesus was going to position Himself as king over Israel. When that change did not happen immediately, the people were disappointed. This was because they expected a Messiah and King to overcome the Roman government, who was occupying the territory at the time. They believed that Israel would be restored again as a kingdom on earth. So one day they asked Jesus about this. They were waiting for Him to restore Israel.

"So when the apostles were with Jesus, they kept asking him, 'Lord, has the time come for you to free Israel and restore our kingdom?' He replied, 'The Father alone has the authority to set those dates and times, and they are not for you to know. But you will receive power when the Holy Spirit comes upon you. And you will be my witnesses, telling people about me everywhere—in Jerusalem, throughout Judea, in Samaria, and to the ends of the earth Acts 1:6-8 NLT).' "

The disciples did not have a clear picture about the plan of God. Jesus directed them and told them that they were going to receive power from on High when the Holy Spirit came upon them. He also told them that they were not to know the set times and dates about the Kingdom on earth. Only the Father knows those set times and dates. Instead, Jesus redirected them to a specific event which turns out to be a wonderful Meeting Place with God: the baptism of the Holy Spirit.

HEAVENLY VISITATION

"But when the Helper comes, whom I shall send to you from the Father, the Spirit of truth who proceeds from the Father, He will testify of Me. And you also will bear witness, because you have been with Me from the beginning (John 15:26-27 emphasis added)."

As believers, we all need to have an experience with the Holy Spirit. This is not just a one time thing, such as what happened after Jesus ascended. This is part of our special meeting place with God where we experience power from on high so that we can fulfill our destiny and purpose in Him.

Jesus promised us that He would send the Holy Spirit to

help us and be with us. In that way, we would never be orphans. The Holy Spirit is the "Spirit of Truth" according to Jesus. He said, "However, when He, the Spirit of truth, has come, He will guide you into all truth; for He will not speak on His own authority, but whatever He hears He will speak; and He will tell you things to come. He will glorify Me, for He will take of what is Mine and declare it to you. All things that the Father has are Mine. Therefore I said that He will take of Mine and declare it to you (John 16:13-16)."

In the Book of Acts, the disciple Luke mentions the events that took place initially and what is still happening today. Luke recalls, "When the Day of Pentecost had fully come, they were all with one accord in one place. And suddenly there came a sound from heaven, as of a rushing mighty wind, and it filled the whole house where they were sitting. Then there appeared to them divided tongues, as of fire, and one sat upon each of them. And they were all filled with the Holy Spirit and began to speak with other tongues, as the Spirit gave them utterance (Acts 2:1-4 emphasis added)."

HERE ARE SOME KEY CHARACTERISTCS OF THIS HOLY SPIRIT VISITATION.

1. The people were in one accord.
2. There was a sound from heaven.
3. There was a rushing, mighty wind.
4. The wind filled the whole house.
5. There appeared to them, separate tongues, as of fire.
6. They were all filled with the Holy Spirit.
7. They all began to speak with other tongues.
8. The Spirit is the One who gave them utterance.

PETER'S TESTIMONIES

It is interesting to note that there are several things that happened when the Holy Spirit fell. The Apostle Peter was preaching to a crowd. The people noticed that after they heard the Word of God, one of the signs of the Spirit falling was that they began to speak with other tongues and worship and magnify God. "While Peter was still speaking these words, the Holy Spirit fell upon all those who heard the Word. And those of the circumcision who believed were astonished, as many as came with Peter, because the gift of the Holy Spirit had been poured out on the Gentiles also. For they heard them speak with tongues and magnify God (Acts 10:44-46)."

Another characteristic of the Holy Spirit's appearance was that the people began repenting of their sins and were baptized in water. "As I began to speak, Peter continued, the Holy Spirit fell on them, just as He fell on us at the beginning. Then I thought of the Lord's words when he said, 'John baptized with water, but you will be baptized with the Holy Spirit.' And since God gave these Gentiles the same gift He gave us when we believed in the Lord Jesus Christ, who was I to stand in God's way? When the others heard this, they stopped objecting and began praising God. They said, 'We can see that God has also given the Gentiles the privilege of repenting of their sins and receiving eternal life' (Acts 11:15-18 NLT)."

SIGNS AND WONDERS

Remember that the Lord will confirm His Word with signs following (see Acts 14:3). You can expect God to meet you when the Word of God is spoken by the Holy Spirit. He will invade your environment and things will begin to happen. God always validates His Word. The Holy Spirit wants to bring attention to Jesus and speak the truth about Him. The writer of Hebrews explains this very well.

How shall we escape if we neglect so great a salvation, which at the first began to be spoken by the Lord, and was confirmed to us by those who heard Him, God also bearing witness both with signs and wonders, with various miracles, and gifts of the Holy Spirit, according to His own will? Hebrews 2:3-4

The Holy Spirit is greater than the spirit that is in the world. He is with us and in us. Yield to Him today, and enter this wonderful meeting place with God. Begin to speak out the Word of God to your environment. You are a overcomer and God wants to say some things through you. He wants to confirm those things which He would have you to speak.

It is good to know that the Holy Spirit will protect you from error in your meeting place. Above all else, pray in the Holy Spirit as you put the Word of God first. We are God's children, and He is a protective Father. The Apostle John said, "You are of God, little children, and have overcome them, because He who is in you is greater than he who is in the world. They are of the world. Therefore they speak as of the world, and the world hears them. We are of God. He who knows God hears us; he who is not of God does not hear us. By this we know the spirit of truth and the spirit of error (1 John 4:4-6)."

Chapter 10

Entering Into the Faith Rest

And to whom did He swear that they would not enter His rest, but to those who did not obey? So we see that they could not enter in because of unbelief.
Hebrews 3:18,19

We need to enter into faith with God and find rest. There is a meeting place with God where your trust in God and the experience then carries you into the rest. Your destiny is secure here because you trust Him now more that ever. Never doubt Him. He loves and cares for you.

FAITH THAT PLEASES

When you meet with God in the "Faith Rest", your whole being is satisfied with the promises of God. You will know that your destiny and purpose are secure. By faith, many people have entered in to an area of pleasing God. In fact, one such person was Enoch.

"Faith lifted Enoch from this life and he was taken up into heaven! He never had to experience death; he just disappeared from this world because God promoted him. For before he was translated to the heavenly realm his life had become a pleasure to God. And without faith living within us it would be impossible to please God. For we come to God in faith knowing that He is real and that He rewards the faith of those who truly seek Him   (Hebrews 11:5,6 TPT)."

The prophet Enoch is mentioned as a great man of faith because his faith had developed to such an extent that there was no resistance to the Word and will of God in his life. He found the Meeting Place with God. He found himself in faith, rest, and trust for the Lord that God allowed Enoch to walk over into the spirit realm one day and never come back. He had a testimony that he pleased God so much that God promoted him. He is mentioned as an example to follow as we journey to our destiny and purpose. The writer of Hebrews encourages us to enter in right now:

Therefore, since a promise remains of entering His rest, let us fear lest any of you seem to have come short of it. For indeed the gospel was preached to us as well as to them; but the word which they heard did not profit them, not being mixed with faith in those who heard it (Hebrews 4:1,2).

MOST HOLY FAITH

One activity that is effective for building you up in your Most Holy faith is praying in tongues. The Apostle Paul interchanges the phrasing "praying in the Spirit" with "praying in tongues" (see Ephesians 6:18; Romans 8:26; and 1 Corinthians 14: 15 for examples). In the footnotes of the Jude 1:20 TPT translation, it gives other phrases such as "Pray as led by the Spirit," "Pray in the Spirit's realm," or "Pray by means of the power of the Spirit."

The wording in Jude 1:20 seems to reflect a constant, and

increasingly productive form of building up your faith. The Apostle Paul was so conviced of this activity that he said, "I thank my God I speak with tongues more than you all (1 Corinthians 14:18)."

"But you, my delightfully loved friends, constantly and progressively build yourselves up on the foundation of your most holy faith by praying every moment in the Spirit (Jude 1:20 TPT)."

Your faith is as precious as gold that is tried in the fire of adversity. It is pure and holy. I have had numerous visitations after I have stood in faith persistently for periods of time in the faith rest. I did not see the manifestation of it physically, but I knew I had it because my faith was proven. I am not basing my faith on how quickly the answer may manifest. I know that in my meeting place with God, I will receive when I exercise faith and rest in Him. I know I will possess whatever my request may be. This is your destiny and purpose in your Promise Land. Go ahead and enter in to it now by faith. Peter understood what we would endure as we enter into our faith rest. He said, "So be truly glad. There is wonderful joy ahead, even though you have to endure many trials for a little while. These trials will show that your faith is genuine. It is being tested as fire tests and purifies gold—though your faith is far more precious than mere gold. So when your faith remains strong through many trials, it will bring you much praise and glory and honor on the day when Jesus Christ is revealed to the whole world. You love Him even though you have never seen Him. Though you do not see Him now, you trust Him; and you rejoice with a glorious, inexpressible joy. The reward for trusting Him will be the salvation of your souls (1 Peter 1:6-9 NLT emphasis added)."

I was supernaturally sent back from death to help inspire and activate people to develop a relationship that possesses great trust in the Lord. We all have a destiny and purpose. We have to receive it spiritually before we can see it physically. In these wonderful times of meeting with God, our trust in Him is cultivated by His love and faithful watchfulness over us. We do not need to worry about anything! Praise His name. May the power of God overshadow you as you meet with Him right now.

Father,

In the name of Jesus we come to you. Thank you for providing us with revelation knowledge concerning your Word. Thank you also for the Holy Spirit who has been sent to explain the truth written in Your Word and to show us the realm of the Spirit. Thank you for this meeting place called Faith Rest. Thank You for taking us all into our destiny and purpose. We are fulfilling what you have written for us within our books in Heaven. May what you have conceived in those books come to pass on earth this day. In Jesus' name,

Amen.

ABOUT THE AUTHOR

Kevin Zadai was called to ministry at the age of ten. He attended Central Bible College in Springfield, Missouri, where he received a Bachelor of Arts in Theology. Later, he received training in Missions at Rhema Bible College. He is currently ordained through Rev. Dr. Jesse and Rev. Dr. Cathy Duplantis. At age thirty-one, during a routine day surgery, he found himself on the 'other side of the veil' with Jesus. For forty-five minutes, the Master revealed spiritual truths before returning him to his body and assigning him to a supernatural ministry. Kevin holds a Commercial Pilot license and has been employed by Southwest Airlines for twenty-nine years as a flight attendant. He and his lovely wife, Kathi, reside in New Orleans, Louisiana.

SALVATION PRAYER

LORD GOD,
I CONFESS THAT I AM A SINNER. I
CONFESS THAT I NEED YOUR SON
JESUS. PLEASE FORGIVE ME IN HIS
NAME.

LORD JESUS, I BELIEVE YOU
DIED FOR ME AND THAT YOU ARE
ALIVE AND LISTENING TO ME NOW.

I NOW TURN FROM MY SINS, AND
WELCOME YOU INTO MY HEART.
COME AND TAKE CONTROL OF MY
LIFE. MAKE ME THE KIND OF
PERSON YOU WANT ME TO BE.

NOW, FILL ME WITH YOUR HOLY
SPIRIT, WHO WILL SHOW ME HOW
TO LIVE FOR YOU. I
ACKNOWLEDGE YOU BEFORE MEN
AS MY SAVIOR AND MY LORD.

IN JESUS' NAME.
AMEN.

IF YOU PRAYED THIS PRAYER. PLEASE CONTACT US AT
info@warriornotes.com for more information and material.

Please look for the companion
study guide and prayer guide for this particular
book. This is volume one of the Heavenly
Encounters Series.

Go to warriornotes.com for other exciting ministry
materials.

Warriornotes.com

Made in the USA
San Bernardino, CA
09 July 2017